Approximate Translation:
Media, Narrative, and Experience in Urban Design

Jonathan Jae-an Crisman

APPLIED
RESEARCH
+DESIGN
PUBLISHING

Published by Applied Research and Design Publishing, an imprint of ORO Editions.
Gordon Goff: Publisher

www.appliedresearchanddesign.com
info@appliedresearchanddesign.com

Author: Jonathan Jae-an Crisman
Cover Design: Jonathan Jae-an Crisman
Book Design: Ly Tran
Project Manager: Jake Anderson

10 9 8 7 6 5 4 3 2 1 First Edition

ISBN: 978-1-954081-50-5

Color Separations and Printing: ORO Editions Inc.
Printed in China.

AR+D Publishing makes a continuous effort to minimize the overall carbon footprint of its publications. As part of this goal, AR+D, in association with Global ReLeaf, arranges to plant trees to replace those used in the manufacturing of the paper produced for its books. Global ReLeaf is an international campaign run by American Forests, one of the world's oldest nonprofit conservation organizations. Global ReLeaf is American Forests' education and action program that helps individuals, organizations, agencies, and corporations improve the local and global environment by planting and caring for trees.

Table of Contents

Alvarado Street in Los Angeles with street vendors, the classic Langer's Deli, and MacArthur Park all in view. Source: author.

Introduction: Media for an Urban Massage

Chapter 1

I live in Los Angeles. One of the main north-south roads in the city is called Alvarado Street. This street looks like any other on a map: a straight line. But that line belies the reality on the ground—Alvarado Street is known as a locus for the immigrant life and culture that makes LA so distinct. A mundane straight line on a map when traversed in person is transformed. The street pulses with a vibrant hustle. People who have made this city their home have transformed this stretch of road: some make their way up and down this street, others have opened storefronts, and others still set up shop right on the sidewalk. The sidewalk itself is more a kind of linear agora than a path for mobility; shops' wares spill out their front doors, while street vendors chat with customers, blurring the lines between interior and exterior, between public and private.

The urban plan, with its neat lines and systematic designations, can't capture the essence of this living, breathing, joyously smelly thing we call the city. How could such a sterile thing on paper capture a serendipitous encounter with friends and acquaintances on the street, or the kaleidoscope of colors, sounds, and smells that present themselves to one's senses? The map lacks the soul of the street. Cities—and, in turn, urban design—are not just about the arrangement of buildings, roads, and public spaces. They are about narratives, experiences, and an element of chance—things that can't be captured by lines on a piece of paper.

And so, with this book, I explore these dimensions of urban life often overlooked by planners and designers. Moreover, I hope to share some practices that can be used by urban designers to move beyond staid urban plans and toward more fully living visions for the future of our cities.

You hold in your hands a demonstration—a proof of concept—of how to do urban design using ideas from media and literary studies and the often under-appreciated design tactics found in strip malls, theme parks, and nightlife. You can read this book as a book—that is to say, as a creative work primarily for entertainment, edification, and visual stimulation. Or, you can use this as a how-to guide for a different kind of urban design. This is all also an experiment; to move from urban design to media studies, to theme park design and back again requires a process that I call "approximate translation." The outcome of a work in translation isn't ever the "right answer" so much as *an* answer—the result of a process of trying things out, testing, experimentation, and failure, like writing an essay (which comes from the French *essayer* for "to try"). Give it a whirl!

Marshall McLuhan's Middle Meddling

In *Kissing Architecture*, Sylvia Lavin develops a theory of "confounding mediums" in which architecture transcends conventional modes of expression when it—particularly its surfaces—is transgressed by another medium.[1] Can this theory be understood at the urban scale? Urban environments have aspects beyond architectural surfaces that demand transgression. Urban signage, with its unique semiotic structure, is an aspect that cannot be understood on the same terms as the surface. Urban spaces are also composed of rich sound- and smell-scapes that offer a means for confounding. And urban space occurs in place: its social and temporal aspects create stories. In other words, this urbanized version of Lavin's theory may hold promise, but only if we expand beyond the architectural surface. The ur-media theorist Marshall McLuhan offers an expanded version of Lavin's insight:

> *All media work us over completely. They are so pervasive in their personal, political, economic, aesthetic, psychological, moral, ethical, and social consequences that they leave no part of us untouched, unaffected, or unaltered. The medium is the massage. Any understanding of social and cultural change is impossible without a knowledge of the way media work as environments.*[2]

Indeed, Lavin obliquely hints at this possibility. She states that what the work of artist Pipilotti Rist "offers to architecture stems not so much from the particular content of Rist's work but from her use of a medium."[3] As McLuhan's widely-quoted aphorism states, the medium is the message—or, at least part of it. If Lavin's theory on conflating mediums is not based on content but, rather, the formal properties of a medium itself, it would logically extend beyond architecture and projection toward all forms of media. In the case of urban environments, their structure is more complex and dynamic than architecture (indeed, architecture is subsumed within the urban environment) and this complexity and dynamism are matched by a number of kissable aspects beyond the architectural surface. So, it would seem that an urban version of Lavin's theory might not involve a kiss but, rather, a full-body massage.

This massage is timely: urban systems are knotty and tense. Design theorists Horst Rittel and Melvin Webber describe many of the complexities and problems facing urban areas as "wicked" in contrast to the "tame" problems that other disciplines solve.[4] While the sciences can work toward discrete solutions through controlled experiments, planning problems have no clear definition, are not immediately testable, and lack enumerable solution sets, among other distinctions that Rittel and Webber describe—how does one address, say, questions of environmental justice, long-term energy provision, or the evaporation of public space? An urban massage offers a multi-valent, fuzzy means through which one can begin to move beyond description and critique of urban conditions and toward action upon them.[5] Of course, prior to utilizing a massage methodology, one must understand the pressure points of an urban environment. One way to do this (in true wicked problem form, though there are likely other means to this end) would be to have an urban model that highlights the particularly kissable or mediatic aspects of such environments.

1 Sylvia Lavin, *Kissing Architecture* (Princeton: Princeton University Press, 2011), 30.

2 Marshall McLuhan and Quentin Fiore, *The Medium is the Massage: An Inventory of Effects* (New York: Bantam Books, 1967), 26.

3 Lavin, *Kissing Architecture*, 23.

4 Horst W. J. Rittel and Melvin M. Webber, "Dilemmas in a General Theory of Planning," *Policy Sciences* 4 (1973): 155-169, https://doi.org/10.1007/BF01405730.

5 See the literature on fuzzy logic by Lotfi Zadeh et al.

There is already at least one structure that offers a microcosm of the urban, requires the discipline of architecture, and is particularly prone to the confounding of media: the theme park. Theme parks offer a controlled, constructed environment in which urbanism and architecture are intentionally conflated with narrative, sensorial, affective, experiential, and graphic media. As design critic Michael Sorkin and others have bemoaned, the city has already become some version of a theme park as the Disneyland-ification and McDonald-ization of the world has set in, courtesy of the forces of globalization.[6] These claims are generally critical and, indeed, there is cause for concern insofar as dream factories like Disney are complicit in the forces of neoliberal capital, privatizing the last vestiges of public space. And the evaporation of public space may be the issue par excellence as a subject of inquiry and target of intervention. It is an age-old question and one particularly relevant at the contemporary moment with the rise, hiccup, and continuing strength of neoliberal capital through the 2008 economic crisis.[7] As architect Rem Koolhaas has written, Singapore may be the quintessential manifestation of this ongoing trend in its uniquely extreme conflation of state interests and global capital toward its aims of ultra-rapid development and modernization, resulting in "the generic city," or what could be seen as an entire urban sphere of content-vacant surfaces waiting to be kissed (and presently impregnated with the products of global capital):

Singapore is perhaps the first semiotic state, a Barthian slate, a clean synthetic surface, a field at once active and neutralized where political themes or minimal semantic particles can be launched and withdrawn, tested like weather balloons. Singapore is run according to Machiavellian semantics—not in an attempt to decode what already exists but as a prospective construction of political meaning.[8]

Koolhaas goes on to describe the development of Singapore by quoting Fumihiko Maki, the Metabolist thinker who helped develop the city's urban form and claimed with regard to his formal ideology, "the most important factor in group form . . . [is] the treating of mediating public spaces."[9] In the end, Koolhaas claims that Singapore still suffers from a "Promethean hangover, . . . grasping for new themes, new metaphors, new signs to superimpose on its luxurious substance."[10] Singapore is waiting to be the poster child for city-as-theme-park but it is, as it stands, just generic space, a park with no theme. Singapore's founding father, Lee Kuan Yew, brokered a Faustian bargain for his city-state: it became an entrepot in the global flow of capital, giving up a sense of place in exchange for the Asian economic miracle. State control over the various mediatic entities in Singapore is typified by Temasek Holdings, the state-owned investment company formerly run by Ho Ching, wife of longtime Prime Minister Lee Hsien Loong. Temasek owns Mediacorp, the largest media broadcaster in Singapore, as well as Singapore Telecommunications, the largest internet, mobile, and phone provider in Singapore. With confounding mediums comes unsolicited intervention—as Rist sensually suggests, invoking a smooch on Yoshio Yaniguchi, architect of the Museum of Modern Art in which her *Pour Your Body Out (7354 Cubic Meters)* was installed in 2008—and such a kiss cannot occur through the vehicle of top-down, state-controlled media enterprises.[11] The entrepreneurial architect or planner—what architect Markus Miessen might call a "crossbench practitioner"—is a necessary agent for performing an urban massage.[12]

6 Michael Sorkin, ed., *Variations on a Theme Park: The New American City and the End of Public Space* (New York: The Noonday Press, 1992).

7 For a good survey of its historiography, see *OASE* 71.

8 Rem Koolhaas, "Singapore Songlines: Portrait of a Potemkin Metropolis . . . or Thirty Years of Tabula Rasa," in *S,M,L,XL* (New York: The Monacelli Press, 1995), 1039.

9 Fumihiko Maki quoted in Koolhaas, "Singapore Songlines," 1049.

10 Koolhaas, "Singapore Songlines," 1077.

11 Lavin, *Kissing Architecture*, 1-4.

12 See Kenny Cupers and Markus Miessen, "Participation and/or Criticality? Thoughts on an Architectural Practice for Urban Change," in "Socio–," ed. Jonathan Crisman, special issue, *Thresholds* 40 (2012): 109, https://doi.org/10.1162/thld_a_00138.

Snapshots from Singapore, a relatively recently developed themed land. Source: author.

Clearly, notions of theming and mediation hold sway over the nature of urban issues and, in particular, public space.[13] But do theme parks offer a means for an urban massage when analyzed purely on formal (i.e., divorced from its political) terms? If so, such an understanding may offer means for fighting fire with fire, for creating public space in the face of global capital with the very tools that it unwittingly created. Indeed, as Koolhaas suggests, these urban spaces devoid of a public sphere are gasping for new content, and should that content be presented through a confounding medium, they may be capable of transcending conventional modes of expression as Lavin's theory dictates. Here, we are offered with the possibility for a kind of humane urban design through a dark alchemy with the products of late capital itself.

Furthermore, theme parks (and their spiritual cousins, strip malls and nightlife spaces) operate on populist terms. The use of their formal properties affords an easy path toward "wide release"—a necessity when dealing with something as massive as public space. While cultural critics Theodor Adorno and Max Horkheimer have long since implicated popular culture as a means through which the masses can be controlled by market interests, figures like architectural theorist Mark Jarzombek have already claimed the realization of Adorno and Horkheimer's fears—that high culture would be tainted by the wiles of mass media—sounded the death knell for other supposed "high" or "critical" modes of cultural production, particularly architecture, and called for the embrace of the death of culture through the championing of Pop.[14, 15] And why not? Why shouldn't an intelligent reanimation of the corpse of cultural production allow the reverse, for the markets to be controlled by mass interests? As Margaret King has described, Disneyland's success came with an intentional shift from amusement park to theme park, "embodying critical shared cultural values as embedded in history, innovation, adventure, and fantasy."[16] Furthermore, the process by which this occurred was by making "the invisible and abstract concrete." In other words, spatializing the popular imagination through a mediatic appliqué on urban form.[17] More recently, capitalist media behemoths like Disney have relied more and more heavily on bottom-up creators and fan-driven activism, driving decision-making in the opposite direction.[18]

13 Perhaps we might think of "public space" as a hyperobject, a thing with such vast spatial and temporal dimension as to make it a "wicked problem"—to use Timothy Morton's term, which I have also used in the past to describe "the city." See Timothy Morton, *Hyperobjects: Philosophy and Ecology after the End of the World* (Minneapolis: University of Minnesota Press, 2013); Dana Cuff, Anastasia Loukaitou-Sideris, Todd Presner, Maite Zubiaurre, and Jonathan Jae-an Crisman, *Urban Humanities: New Practices for Reimagining the City* (Cambridge: MIT Press, 2020).

14 Max Horkheimer and Theodor W. Adorno, "The Culture Industry: Enlightenment as Mass Deception," in *Dialectic of Enlightenment* (New York: Herder and Herder, 1972), 120–167.

15 Mark Jarzombek, "ECO-POP: In Praise of Irony, Hyperbole, and Readymades," *Cornell Journal of Architecture* 8 (2011): 58–62. Several of the articles in *Perspecta* 40 (2008) are also worth looking at, building upon the notion of contemporary cultural and architectural production's zombie-esque, undead nature.

16 Margaret J. King, "The Disney Effect: Fifty Years After Theme Park Design," in *Disneyland and Culture: Essays on the Parks and Their Influence*, ed. Kathy Merlock Jackson and Mark I. West (Jefferson: McFarland, 2011), 225.

17 Ibid., 226.

18 See, for example, the classic *Textual Poachers: Television Fans & Participatory Culture* by Henry Jenkins (London: Routledge, 1992) or any of the other work coming from fan studies today.

Pop in the Production of Public Space

While the joys of Pop are easy to sell, the nature of contemporary cultural production complicates its pithy, popular, PR perception. When Pop went high culture, starting with the 1956 *This Is Tomorrow* exhibition at the Whitechapel Art Gallery in London, it began the process of wiping clean the visage of art from its avant-garde face paint.[19] But today we are at a point where the vacuity of art, or at least its complicity in the machine of global capital, is widely acknowledged, as Jarzombek and others suggest. The boundary between high and low has been all but erased, leaving, at best, a blurry reminder of its former existence. The complications of Pop today, rather, are what Kazys Varnelis describes as "network culture." With the ease of knowledge transfer enabled by the Internet, Varnelis cites Nicholas Bourriaud's observation that artists "don't really 'create' anymore, they reorganize."[20] What's more, the distinction between artist and viewer has collapsed with the rise of participatory media:

> *In the case of art and architecture, Jameson suggests, a widespread reaction to the elitism of the modern movement and the new closeness between capital and culture led to the rise of aesthetic populism. Network culture exacerbates this condition as well, dismissing the populist projection of the audience's desires onto art for the production of art by the audience and the blurring of boundaries between media and the public. If appropriation was a key aspect of postmodernism, network culture almost absentmindedly uses remix as its dominant process.*[21]

19 Institute for Art and Urban Resources, *This Is Tomorrow Today: The Independent Group and British Pop Art* (New York: Institute for Art and Urban Resources, 1987).

20 Nicholas Bourriaud, "Public Relations," interview by Bennett Simpson, *ArtForum,* April 2001.

If the contemporary condition is such that even participatory media is complicit within the system of global capital, some kind of subversion of Pop media must allow for an escape. And, like the convenient existence of the theme park—again, other possibilities probably exist, the strip mall and nightclub among them—there already exists a process by which Pop can be subverted: surrealism. The subconscious, anti-rational, nonconformist manifesto laid out by André Breton in 1924 describes the machinery necessary for subverting neoliberal capital long before it ever set in as the dominant political economic structure of our time.[22] It both flies in the face of the hyperrationality of global capital and can fill up its tank with the unconscious mass sensibility responsible for Pop. Its history is littered with examples that seem to be some kind of populist dream, revealing the psychological realities of mass fears and hopes. Furthermore, its method is the network culture mash-up: surrealist work takes the images of our mind and represents them in tangible form, revealing their true natures through photoshopping—image filters, free transformation, and layering.

21 Kazys Varnelis, "Conclusion: The Meaning of Network Culture," in *Networked Publics*, ed. Kazys Varnelis (Cambridge: MIT Press, 2008), 150.

22 André Breton, *Manifestoes of Surrealism* (Ann Arbor: University of Michigan Press, 1969).

Not coincidentally, new popular movements of street art have been called "Neo-Pop" and "Pop Surrealism," a clear mode of conflating mediums.[23] Utilizing the Pop method of repetition, Pop Surrealism took its task as "repeatedly and incessantly producing a meme about which opinion, good or ill, could be voiced in the marketplace of ideas."[24] In repeating mediatic forms across urban space, in copy-pasting and photoshopping new narratives onto old structures of capital, one seems to gain a certain efficacy through sheer volume. And using Pop's love for low culture, "Pop Surrealism is defined in part by a generation whose influences are not primarily those of fine art's world—they consist of video games, Bugs Bunny, Saturday morning television ads masquerading as education, and the increasing allure of cheap, limitless entertainments."[25] The precious material of an unequal mass media production power structure is ripe territory for subversion, indeed.

Pop Surrealism's development also offers a site of intervention, a testbed for experimentation: Los Angeles. Beyond the obvious correlation between LA, media empires, and Disney, as Karnowsky describes, "Pop Surrealism's 'ground zero' might be most easily traced back to curator Paul Schimmel's 1992 MOCA exhibition *Helter Skelter: L. A. Art in the 1990s*, a collection that included pieces by Robert Williams and a trio of artists who continue to make solid and meaningful inroads into fine art, Paul McCarthy, Mike Kelly, and Raymond Pettibon."[26] Other key figures in the movement who operate out of California are Gary Baseman, who began his career in Disney's studios, and Tim Biskup. And as far as the rigor of an urban study is concerned, Los Angeles invites analysis insofar as it's been implicated, connected, and described ad infinitum with relation to urban theory, the world city hypothesis, and analytical methodologies at large by the so-called LA School, including figures like Mike Davis and Edward Soja, and by those influenced by Michel de Certeau's ideas on "the everyday," such as Margaret Crawford and John Chase.[27] With a methodology as nascent as the kiss—to say nothing of the massage—such a grounded intellectual background is a necessity.

23 Julie Kogler and Giorgio Calcara, eds., *Apocalypse Wow! Pop Surrealism, Neo Pop, Urban Art* (Milan: Silvana Editoriale, 2009).

24 Merry Karnowsky, "Pop Surrealism at the Ends of the Earth," in *Apocalypse Wow! Pop Surrealism, Neo Pop, Urban Art*, ed. Julie Kogler and Giorgio Calcara (Milan: Silvana Editoriale, 2009), 95.

25 Ibid.

26 Ibid.

27 Mike Davis, *City of Quartz: Excavating the Future in Los Angeles* (London: Verso, 1990); Edward W. Soja, *Postmodern Geographies: The Reassertion of Space in Critical Social Theory* (London: Verso, 1989); Michel de Certeau, *The Practice of Everyday Life* (Berkeley: University of California Press, 1984); John Chase, Margaret Crawford, and John Kaliski, *Everyday Urbanism* (New York: The Monacelli Press, 1999).

To summarize, I propose conflating mediums at the urban scale based on learning from theme parks, and Los Angeles more generally. Rather than the kissing of architectural surface and video projection, I propose the mixing of urban aspects with a variety of media: a full-body massage. You can think of this massage as a kind of translation—but rather than the transformation of a text from one language to another, here we move from one structured set of urban media to another. This is the process of approximate translation in urban design.

What Is Approximate Translation?

All translations are, to some degree, approximate. They are acts of biased, inspired, or perhaps uninspired interpretation.[28] The best one-to-one translation of a word might have a perfectly accurate denotation but still lack a comprehensive set of respective connotations. And this is to say nothing of translations that must deal with lexical gaps, variations in syntax, and outright error. Nevertheless, one can find translations that somehow manage to be even more clear, poetic, and true than their originals. The key is not in surface-level semantic accuracy or even structural integrity, but, rather, in a devotion to maintaining the meaning and experience that affect a reader. The same is true for non-verbal translations—the shift of meaning or experience from one medium to another, the transposition of a space from one place to another, or for the revelation of events from one time into another. In other words, one might translate the rainforest into a restaurant, or Ancient Greece into a Tennessee destination, and despite the obvious errors in translation, its approximate nature nevertheless provides an articulate set of signs and symbols that is of useful value to its readers. Or at least some of them.

28 I use translation in the visual arts sense, as the OED describes, "The expression or rendering of a thing in another medium or form; the conversation or adaptation of a thing to another system, context or use. Also concrete: something created as a result of this process." *Oxford English Dictionary*, s.v. "translation (n.), sense I.3," December 2023, https://doi.org/10.1093/OED/1076190907. But here I also dwell on the more commonly understood sense of translation and all its literary, metaphorical possibility—but, of course, I could not possibly capture all the richness, depth, and knowledge produced through translation studies from Holmes on (though perhaps might suggest Chana Kronfeld as a place for those interested to start). James S. Holmes, "The Name and Nature of Translation Studies," in *Translated! Papers on Literary Translation and Translation Studies* (Amsterdam: Rodopi, 1988), 67–80; Chana Kronfeld, *The Full Severity of Compassion: The Poetry of Yehuda Amichai* (Redwood City: Stanford University Press, 2016).

The Parthenon in Nashville, Tennessee, a full-size replica of the original Parthenon in Athens, Greece, built in 1897 for the Tennessee Centennial Exposition. Photograph by Haines Photo Co., c. 1909. Source: Library of Congress, LC-USZ62-121143.

As a means of testing these claims, this volume includes a series of approximate translations that work toward transforming Allston, a nondescript neighborhood in Boston, into a more certain version of itself. Approximate translation is an urban design strategy meant to make places more themselves, to add definition to the otherwise generic, or perhaps even to combat the pervasive mechanisms of globalization which have gradually evacuated so much of the idiosyncratic from everyday life. These approximate translations are interspersed with explorations of associated ideas, ranging from themed space to platonic forms, that can help us understand how to go about interpretation and design. Namely, chapter 3 dwells on the history and nature of theme parks, exploring how we might learn from them for urban design practice. And Chapter 5 presents ideas on the infinite, no less, and how the Manhattan grid—as Koolhaas has so aptly observed—and Angeleno strip mall can offer insight into how to design cities for diversity, for the unexpected, and more generally how to avoid the imposition of our designerly views on the people for whom we design.

As for the urban design process, in Chapter 2, we start with the first and most widely used approximate translation of a place: simply that of a conventional urban design process in which site, context, and traditional operations of filling and connecting are deployed. We will pay particular attention to the historical palimpsest of Allston, considering how its place-embedded history might influence its design and translation, in addition to its spatial configuration. Next, several new proposed approximate translations are demonstrated, though these are by no means exhaustive of the potential varieties of translation. This book is meant to offer you a way of thinking about urban design interventions such that you might add additional chapters of your own—what is *your* process for approximate translation? Where one ends, another always begins.

For our case study on Allston, we begin with *displacement* in Chapter 4, or the transposition of an urban ecology into a foreign place. The act of displacement compels the translator to understand the source material more fully in its context. What remains, what stays the same—and what is lost—through the removal of contextual noise? As a way of translating the site-specific histories and experiential qualities in Allston, we will turn to the theme park as a teacher. As a strategy for organizing spatial configurations, we will turn to ideal forms, or the most basic of geometries, the line, the circle, the triangle, the square, and so on. These translational tools will allow us to transform Boston-bound Allston into Allstonland, a theme park situated on the site of Hong Kong Disneyland.

Subsequently, of course, this can be re-translated back into its original state through an act of *replacement*, explored in Chapter 6, which brings with it the learnings from the original act of displacement. So much of contemporary critical discourse focuses on deconstruction without sufficient attention to how we ought to reorient our creative capacities. Just as—or perhaps more so—important is the act of reconstruction, of building the world anew. Strategies of style and the infinite possibilities of the grid, and the strip mall, will inform another iteration of approximate translation. And even more so, learning from Plato's platonic ideals can inform yet another urban design strategy that is perhaps so simple it has been often overlooked. Here we will experiment by taking our experience-laden theme park and reinserting it back into Boston, creating New Allston.

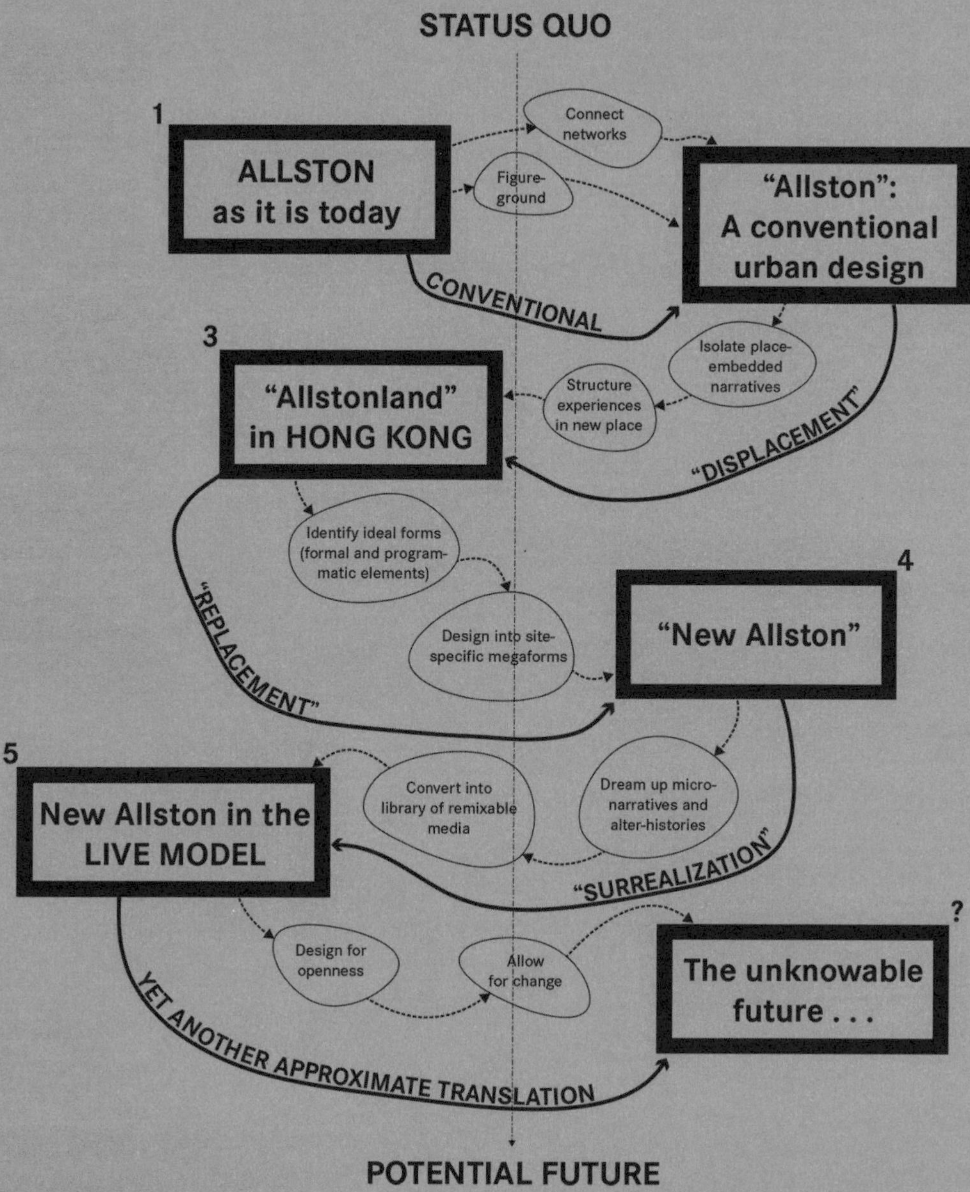

Diagram of the proposed urban design process of approximate translation for Allston. Source: author.

And, finally, there is *surrealization*, or the layering of conflicting naratives and perceptions of a place into a synthetic whole that adheres to the subconscious interpretations we have of that place, which we explore in Chapter 8. Despite their apparent irrationality, these mediated representations of place can offer more of a sense of place to our sensorium than "rational" and "objective" representations of a place. Attention to narrative and media is important for surrealizing a place, and we will explore the possibility of a new urban modeling technique called the "live model," wherein physical models are layered with sound, image, and video. Most importantly, the live model is live mixed using DJ and VJ equipment to capture and embed the elements of happenstance, experience, and temporality that are so central to our sensing of urban places. We will see New Allston surrealized and transformed into a live model.

In all, as I wrote earlier, I hope this book gives you a newfound appreciation for theme parks, strip malls, and urban history; that it guides and inspires you with a novel set of urban design practices that you can use in your own work; but most of all, that it provides you with a bit of nourishing fun! In the words of the immortalized Auntie Mame: *life is a banquet—and most poor suckers are starving to death!*

Chapter 2

Introducing Allston: An Urban Design for a Boston Neighborhood

Allston, by all external appearances, is a very "normal" neighborhood—as normal as you might find anywhere in America. Like Palms in Los Angeles, a place that I'm more familiar with, it is primarily a residential neighborhood with a few small strips of commercial development that aren't defined by much of anything. Its urban form matches that of the most generic elsewhere in Boston, triple-deckers and row house-style apartments with bay windows. But just beneath its innocuous surface lies a wealth of urban history, idiosyncratic tendencies, and cultural detritus waiting to be revealed.

Allston Village. Photograph by Rich Moffitt, 2008. Source: Flickr (used under CC BY 2.0).

The neighborhood, as it appears, hardly lives up to its namesake, Washington Allston. Allston (the person) was an iconic painter and poet who lived in Cambridge for much of his life, and was known for developing a particularly American sensibility for dramatic vistas and landscapes. Allston (the neighborhood), on the other hand, leaves something to be desired. Depending on which portion of the neighborhood you are in, there is either trash and vomit (probably near Harvard Ave and Comm Ave, from undergrad partiers) or soon-to-be CEOs (around the Harvard School of Business). If any demographic groups are more noticeable in the highly mixed community, it is likely the groups of students and of recent immigrants. International languages abound, particularly down Harvard Ave where a Korean restaurant, a Brazilian salon, and a Russian grocery store abut each other—almost like the setup to a joke. Overall, however, it is largely ignored by development and political programs in Boston as it is perceived to be a shabby but more or less alright neighborhood. It's nothing to write home about, but nothing to worry about either—it can just be ignored.

But the plot thickens. Allston, like most of Boston, has been built on fill, layer after layer of itself. What is now the Beacon Park Yard, and until recently was the CSX Railyard, a huge swath of land that is not even accessible by sight, was formerly the nationally recognized Brighton Park horserace track, and before that, a picturesque landscape surrounded by residential development, and before that, a muddy waste that was more-or-less part of the Charles River. And now it is slated to be eaten up by Harvard University's rapid expansion, which is also happening elsewhere around Lower Allston—named for its elevation, not its latitude—an expansion that happened at the swift stroke of midnight when a swath of wealthy alumni had bought up individual parcels around the neighborhood and deeded them over to the university, flouting the due process of eminent domain. Also cutting through the neighborhood are Mass Pike, which was touted as "the world's most modern superhighway" when it was first proposed in the late 1940s, and the MBTA Green Line which was part of the oldest submerged subway in the nation.

Elsewhere in the neighborhood, WBZ Studios stands as the first commercial radio station in the nation, and the Horace Mann School for the Deaf and Hard of Hearing was home to Alexander Graham Bell when he began to develop the telephone and Helen Keller when she learned to speak. Packard's Corner emerged from Packard's Sales Stable and Riding School and later became one of the first urban auto malls where Boston businessman Alvan Tufts Fuller used the branding to capitalize on a franchise of the Packard Motor Car Company. And most notable in contemporary culture is Allston's alter ego, "Rock City." The neighborhood is home to several important performance venues and has been home to many bands, not least of all Aerosmith.

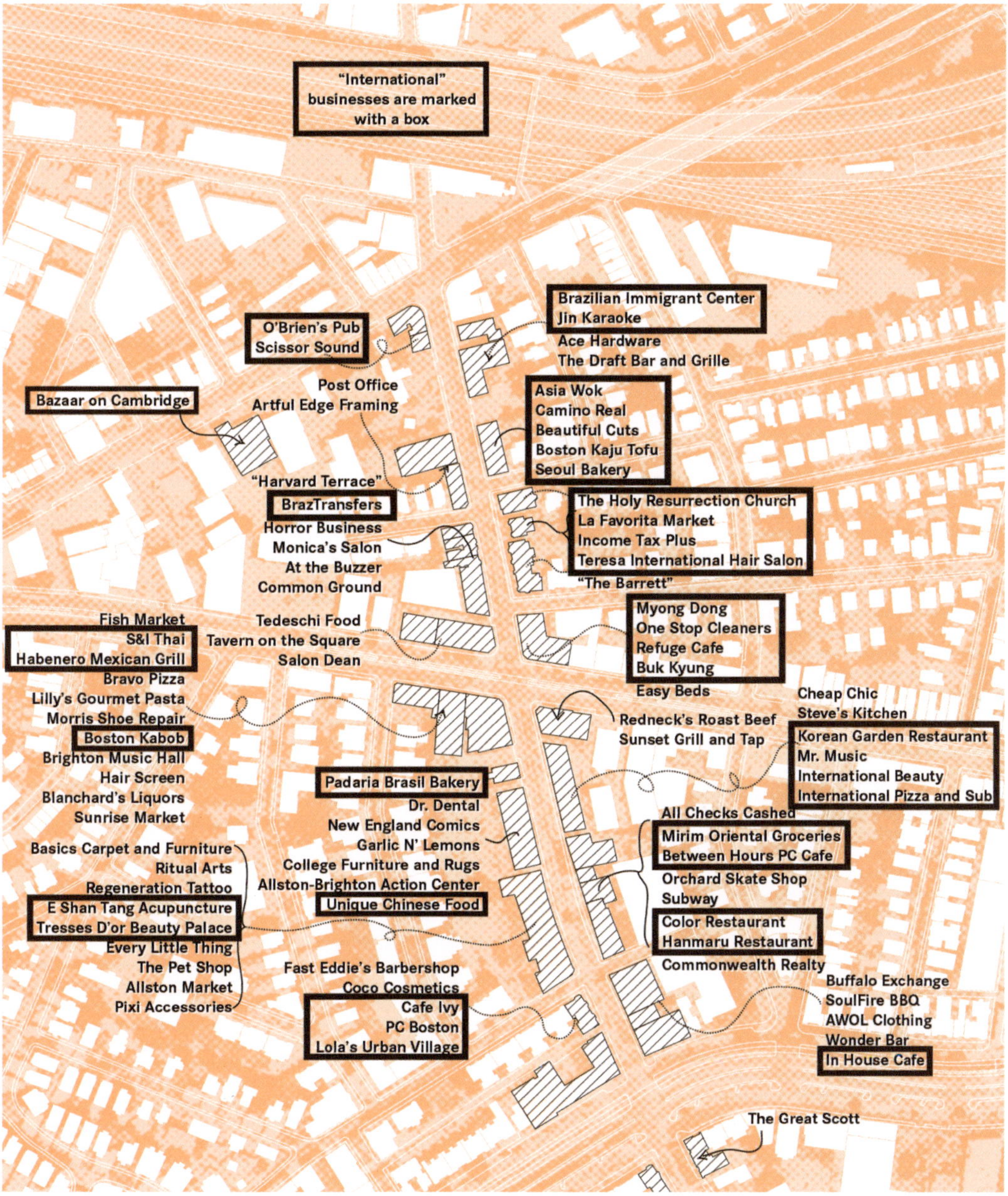

Agglomeration mapping of the cluster of international markets, restaurants, and more in the heart of Allston. All businesses are listed while international establishments are marked with a box. Source: author.

Mark Jarzombek, in his monograph on "Urban Heterology," dismantles the various truth claims and values assumed when operating in urban territory.[1] Notions of objective history, superior authenticity, and apolitical governance are exposed as hypocritical myths that sustain ulterior motives, whether by design or accident. By way of example, Jarzombek references one such mediatized explanation within his object of focus, Dresden: "A Boston newspaper recently proclaimed: 'Dresden Builds a Future: German City Reconstructs its Demolished Past.' It would be more accurate if we were to put every single word of that headline in quotation marks."[2]

The semantic accuracy of properly putting all that is of questionable reality into quotation marks is not the end goal, of course. Would it improve our environment if we were to navigate through a world where every last thing displayed hovering scare quotes (for surely everything has some degree of artifice)? The real translation of those quotation marks into changes within urban space—changes to mediatized perceptions, physical forms, and political positions—is really what is of interest. The moment that Dresden, or any city in question, assumes at the onset a palimpsest reality wherein conflicting histories are simultaneously accepted, micro-narratives are championed over meta-truths, and the political nature of most everything is aired in the open is the moment where we can comfortably ignore claims lacking quotation marks.

Place-embedded History

1 Mark Jarzombek, *Urban Heterology: Dresden and the Dialectics of Post-Traumatic History* (Lund: Lund University, Department of Theoretical and Applied Aesthetics, 2001).

2 Ibid.

Indeed, while Jarzombek's monograph focuses on the situation of Dresden, where many of these issues are in higher relief, it turns out to be uncomfortably applicable in its accusations toward nearly every urban area, not least of all Allston. The shabby neighborhood, so shunned and identified as the college town's college town forwent whatever other narratives might break down this singular identity. Alexander Graham Bell and Helen Keller fade into the shadows and the everyday stories shared through animated oral means across a variety of languages are ignored. But this doesn't have to be the case; one cannot even claim to know what Allston is without an attempt to absorb all this *substance*.

We often call this misappropriated urban substance "local history," though I prefer the term "place-embedded history." It is cultural content that is inextricably linked to a specific place and, as such, constitutes part of that place's reality. One cannot fully understand, let alone even perceive, a place without seeing the totality of its embedded history. And, just as in Dresden, this history is a contentious, layered composition of conflicting narratives, personas, scenarios, might-have-beens, events, politics, and on and on, that nevertheless add up to just one thing: that place. One must work with place-embedded history in a slightly different way from how one typically treats history. Horizontality, fuzziness, and expansiveness are embraced toward the aim of glimpsing, however briefly, totality. Clarity, specificity, and singularity are, while by no means completely out of the question, certainly not ideal—or, perhaps, possible—for an honest aggregate of place-embedded history.

I think here of Hayden White's notion of the "practical past," which stands in contrast to the History of professional historians.[3] Rather than an ever more rarefied approach to writing official histories for the books, we have instead a kind of practical history (White is borrowing philosopher Michael Oakeshott's term here) that is useful for everyday people and their everyday affairs. Ironically, this perhaps gets closer to Benjamin's apocalyptic sense of history given its reality and impact for those of us trying to get by day to day.[4] The truth claims so inherent to "History" are abandoned for something more akin to campfire storytelling where each member, with flickering light cast upon their face, has a chance to contribute the tall tale that was heard from someone else who heard it from someone else. We're just trying to make sense of our surroundings so that we can go about our day with a little more clarity, and hopefully a bit of lively fun. On these terms, Huell Howser stands out as a paragon among historians.

3 Hayden White, *The Practical Past* (Evanston: Northwestern University Press, 2014).

4 "A Klee painting named 'Angelus Novus' shows an angel looking as though he is about to move away from something he is fixedly contemplating. His eyes are staring, his mouth is open, his wings are spread. This is how one pictures the angel of history. His face is turned toward the past. Where we perceive a chain of events, he sees one single catastrophe which keeps piling wreckage and hurls it in front of his feet. The angel would like to stay, awaken the dead, and make whole what has been smashed. But a storm is blowing in from Paradise; it has got caught in his wings with such a violence that the angel can no longer close them. The storm irresistibly propels him into the future to which his back is turned, while the pile of debris before him grows skyward. This storm is what we call progress." Walter Benjamin, "Thesis No. IX," in *Theses on the Philosophy of History* (1940). Translated and published in English in *Illuminations* (New York: Harcourt, Brace & World, 1968).

The MASS PIKE dates back to 1948 and was billed as "The World's Most Modern Superhighway."

The HORACE MANN SCHOOL FOR THE DEAF AND HARD OF HEARING is where Alexander Graham Bell first developed his ideas for the telephone and where Helen Keller first learned to speak.

WASHINGTON ALLSTON is the neighborhood's namesake, an influential American painter and poet. The South Carolinian attended Harvard and traveled the world before spending the last years of his life in Cambridge, Massachusetts.

Allston has also been known as ROCK CITY because of its rich and storied rock history and the numerous music venues including Brighton Music Hall, Paradise Rock Club, the Great Scott, and others.

AEROSMITH penned their first song in an apartment building on Comm Ave where they also had a free 40-year anniversary concert in 2012.

Mapping out key place-embedded histories in Allston. Source: author.

WBZ, based in Allston, was the first commercial radio station in the US and the first commercial television station in New England.

BRAVES FIELD was home to the storied Boston Braves franchise prior to their movement to Milwaukee and subsequently Atlanta. The field was home to several other teams before it was ultimately sold to Boston University and renamed Nickerson Field.

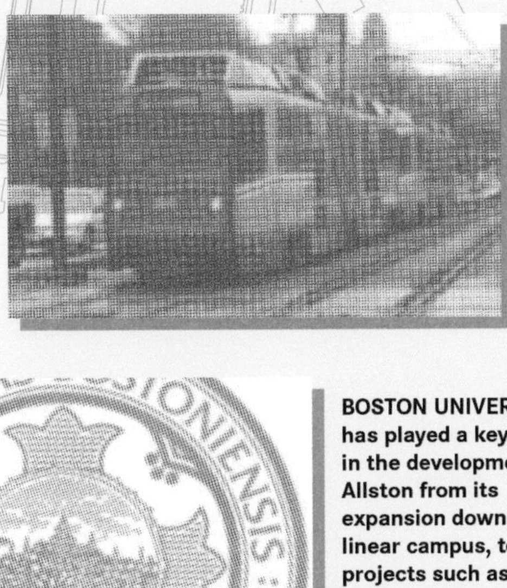

The **GREEN LINE** passes through Allston and it was one of the oldest systems of public transit in the US, including the oldest submerged subway in the nation.

BOSTON UNIVERSITY has played a key role in the development of Allston from its expansion down its linear campus, to projects such as Josep Lluis Sert's Library and Law Tower complex.

PACKARD'S CORNER emerged from Packard's Sales Stable and Riding School and later became one of the first urban auto malls where the Boston businessman Alvan Tufts Fuller used the branding to capitalize on a franchise of the Packard Motor Car Company.

So, what is to be done in this neighborhood that is more or less alright? While it operates just as well as any neighborhood in Boston, its value is tremendously underappreciated, and its populace is similarly at the whims of unfriendly capital and political interests. Not least of all, Harvard University's aggressive expansion threatens to destroy Allston's urban fabric despite well-meaning alterations to its designs. There is also a significant break between Lower Allston where Harvard and more well-to-do residential is located, and the remainder of the neighborhood south of Mass Pike where the students, vomit, and noise provide a lively, if shabby, landscape—and where I lived for a time. The two portions of Allston are riven by the freeway and lack clear pathways of connection.

Two Acts on the Stage of Urban Design

A conventional urban design, in doing due diligence toward improving Allston's quality of life, might find that key arteries between the two portions of the neighborhood could be connected, and the patchwork urban fabric down its central spine might be filled out. Indeed, this potential spine is anchored by Harvard's proposed development around Barry's Corner at the northern end and the active Harvard Ave corridor at the southern end. If a bridge connected development, pedestrian, and vehicular connections across Mass Pike, it could act as an activated boulevard that would unite the disparate elements of the neighborhood and enliven its urban atmosphere.

Indeed, connecting urban networks (roads, paths, and other lines on the landscape) and implementing figure-ground analysis (looking at the patterns of building and open space in an urban plan and filling in or hollowing out accordingly) are two quintessential urban design practices to start with. Let's call these two acts in our stage play of urban design. Each offers much in our quest toward making cities more livable, enjoyable, and productive. Act One: to connect urban networks is to pay attention to the streets, the arteries of a city, to ensure that its inhabitants can move about freely and without interruption. Streets, along with all sorts of other paths—pedestrian paths, bikeways and waterways, and all those other sorts of things that pop up in linear fashion on an urban plan—are the places where mobility is enabled, but also where encounters can happen. A well-connected city is an efficient one, where energy networks are also considered, where alternative futures can be played out. In short, urban networks allow us to consider mobility, along with social, economic, and ecological factors, and are a key tool by which urban designers can consider how people, the natural environment, and built environment impact one another (again, enhanced by new developments in computational analysis).

Conversely, where connecting urban networks focuses on linar pathways, figure-ground analysis focuses on the shapes on an urban plan. It enables our understanding of the buildings, open spaces, neighborhoods, and geography of a city. Act Two: look at these shapes in black and white—no shades of grey—to really understand the spatiality and patterns that make up a place. Look at open spaces in comparison to built spaces, and you can understand a lot. A lot to buy, a lot to sell, a parking lot adjacent a building. You can begin to understand where we ought to build, or where we ought to preserve open space, say, a park for the public. By starting with these two urban design methods, you can accomplish a lot.

First: networks. The origin of the urban design strategy of connecting networks lies in questions of mobility. Integrating new construction with a city's existing infrastructure is generally a key priority; an easily navigable city benefits its residents through access to services, amenities, and social inclusion. Network connectivity also enables transport of labor and goods, so critical in the capitalist city for boosting the economy. It is important to note that here urban networks include not only roadways for automobiles, but the streets, sidewalks, paths, pipes, tubes, and tunnels that allow passage of all kinds of things—most of all, people.

These networks, like arteries in the body, provide life to all they touch: subway stops adjacent shops and street vendors, viewsheds down boulevards to public spaces and buildings, and so on. Cities since Roman times have used grid plans to ensure universal access, while organic urban growth in cities like Paris saw messy urban networks that just wouldn't do. Instead, such places saw their urban fabric violently chopped up by proto-planners like Baron Haussmann, ensuring connections across urban space and enabling the seemingly timeless beauty of Paris that we now take for granted.

But more than just movement, well-connected networks ensure ecological benefits as well. In the Netherlands, the city of Almere has reduced the risk of pluvial flooding from a network of water surface systems, while in China such systems have been used to design its Tianjin Eco-City.[5]

Public health, a field with origins linked to urban planning and studies, has also seen a reinvigorated sensibility toward cities and space after COVID-19 demonstrated the importance of urban networks' impacts on disease spread. In New York City, for example, evidence showed that areas with short commute times and well-mixed and well-distributed points of interest ensured lower rates of disease—urban qualities enabled by robust and thoughtfully designed networks.[6]

The process for urban designers is easy in concept but difficult in practice: one must analyze and examine all urban networks in a context and ensure that new interventions fit neatly into this network—and, ideally, even clean up and improve network robustness. This, of course, requires a significant amount of data, mapping, analysis, and iterative cycles of design. Consider, also, the embodied reality of the line; a line is not only a line, but a material road, a sidewalk, a bike path. How might the cyclist feel if there was no material separation between them and vehicular traffic, for example?

Urban metabolism is another emergent methodology that is deeply intertwined with consideration of urban networks, and offers much to their analysis. Energy flows in, through, and out of a system all occur via networks, and urban systems are no different. Recent developments that shift focus from quantitative analysis toward qualitative and spatial analysis provide an even more robust metric by which one's connective analysis and design can be tested.[7]

5 Zhengnan Zhou, Lei Qu, and Tao Zou, "Quantitative Analysis of Urban Pluvial Flood Alleviation by Open Surface Water Systems in New Towns: Comparing Almere and Tianjin Eco-city," *Sustainability* 7, no.10 (2015): 1-28, https://doi.org/10.3390/su71013378.

6 Yang Yang, Yihong Li Katharina Kral, Nathaniel Hupert, and Timur Dogan, "Urban Design Attributes and Resilience: COVID-19 Evidence from New York City," *Buildings & Cities* 2, no. 1 (2021): 618-636, https://doi.org/10.5334/bc.130.

7 Roberta Pistoni and Sophie Bonin, "Urban Metabolism Planning and Designing Approaches between Quantitative Analysis and Urban Landscape," *City, Territory and Architecture* 4, no. 1 (2017): 1-11, https://doi.org/10.1186/s40410-017-0076-y.

Second: figure-ground. Figure-ground diagrams are commonly used for analysis and design of urban plans, at least since the 19th century. These diagrams map out binaries in urban plans, the most famous being derived from Giambattista Nolli's 1749 map of Rome, which showed its private spaces (typically the interiors of private buildings) in a poche black, while its public spaces (often open streets and squares, but also public interiors such as that of the Pantheon) were left unrendered as voids.

The underlying principle behind figure-ground analysis, though, comes from psychology. Our ability to quickly see, perceive, and analyze figure-ground diagrams has been recognized as a fundamental principle by Gestalt psychologists in the process of human development and visual learning.[8] While their argument that humans had some degree of innately born figure recognition has since been somewhat discredited, our visual processing of figure-ground relationships remains well documented—the classic "Rubin's vase" image of two people looking at each other versus a vase in between them as the ur-example of our immediate ability to process stark figure-ground images, as well as their ability to flip on a dime based on visual analysis.

Figure-ground analysis allows for the rapid understanding of the urban plan on many registers: as built or unbuilt, as public or private, as hardscape or softscape, or any other register for analysis that you might deem relevant to the design at hand. In contrast to urban network analysis which focuses on the line, here figure-ground analysis focuses on two-dimensional shapes in plan such as the figures of buildings, or plazas, and so on. And just like the analysis of urban networks provides a strategy for design through efficient geometric connections, here too we are presented with a strategy for design based on careful connections between two-dimensional shapes as we fill in or excavate out. For example, based on figure-ground analysis, we might determine that a particular city-block is of an odd shape and ought to be filled in based on our geometric analysis, or perhaps we see that two critical public spaces are separated from one another, and we want to excavate out the poche so that public life can be reinvigorated anew.

Urban voids, like large redevelopment sites, are ideal candidates for figure-ground analysis. Designers can learn about preexisting spatial patterns in such areas and use them to inform designs for new development by analyzing the figure-ground relationship of the area. This ensures that the new area blends in well with its surroundings, strengthening the city as a whole.

8 Mary A. Peterson and Emily Skow Grant, "Memory and Learning in Figure-Ground Perception," *Cognitive Vision: Psychology of Learning and Motivation* 42 (2003): 1–34, https://doi.org/10.1016/S0079-7421(03)01001-6.

Plate 5 of 12 from Giovanni Battista Nolli's "New Plan of Rome" (1748), now commonly known as the Nolli Map. It shows a figure-ground mapping of Rome that shows all public spaces, be they exterior such as the streets and plazas, or interior such as the Pantheon or various churches, while private spaces are rendered as poche. Source: Wikimedia Commons.

So, as we turn our gaze back to Allston, we can use these two urban design strategies to great effect. The first and most straightforward approach to analyzing urban networks is to look at the street networks in the neighborhood. Allston's geometric nature is largely vertical; its north-south axis runs from Harvard's holdings in Lower Allston, while the heart of Allston is to its south. The east-west axis is one of neighborhood transition: you move into Brighton toward the west, and Brookline toward the east, with the Charles River providing a hard stop to Boston's edge. Yet this verticality is interrupted. The 90 freeway bisects Lower Allston from Allston, interrupting its continuity. The main streets that continue over the freeway are less than ideal, Everett Street is a smaller non-commercial road, and Cambridge Street is primarily east to west.

Looking at the pattern of lines, however, we can see that Harvard Street, the primary north-south thoroughfare in central Allston terminates at the 90 freeway, with the smaller Franklin Street continuing north of the freeway all the way up and back into a curiously broken Harvard Street as it re-enters the domain of Harvard University in Lower Allston. So a first urban design move would be to reconnect these disparate networks into a single north-south axis as a spine that runs through the whole neighborhood, providing continuity between its parts and most especially across the 90 freeway.

Second, after this move, we can map out the built environment along this spine to perform our figure-ground analysis, here focusing on built spaces and urban voids. We can note larger parcels in the north where Harvard University is located, starts and stops of commercial building along the spine, and a few voids that would make pedestrian life very uncomfortable indeed for a resident navigating down this boulevard. So here our second urban design move will be to focus on filling up these urban voids along the spine to reinforce continuity, transforming the handful of residential buildings along the spine to have some commercial aspect—perhaps completely, or perhaps just at the ground level—and as an added improvement on existing urban conditions, we can even build over the 90 freeway, completely obscuring its dreary existence from view by pedestrians at the ground level.

Opposite page: A perfectly fine urban design plan for Allston using the strategies of connecting networks and figure-ground analysis. Source: author.

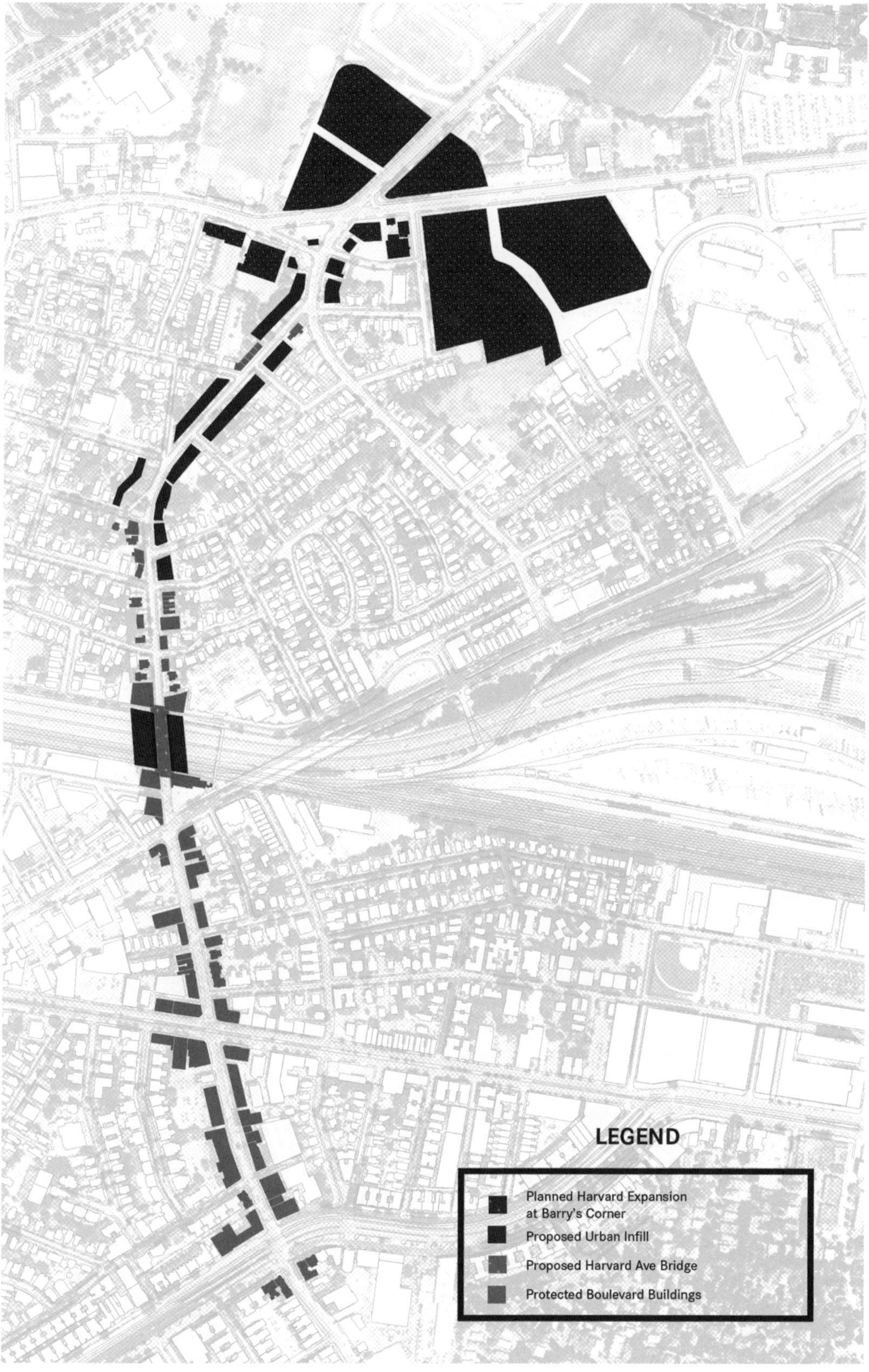
LEGEND
Planned Harvard Expansion at Barry's Corner
Proposed Urban Infill
Proposed Harvard Ave Bridge
Protected Boulevard Buildings

Such an urban design is certainly well-intentioned and would dramatically improve the urban environment. Yet we can do more! This design ignores the structural, social, mediatic, and experiential elements of the urban totality. Without a programmed narrative that is open to its inhabitants, this design would act as little more than an infrastructural upgrade separate from the temporal rhythms and social fabrics latent within Allston.

In the case of Allston, our urban design strategy must embrace the community's distinctive identity and place-embedded history. As we envision connecting urban networks and conducting figure-ground analysis, we should seek to integrate the neighborhood's historical layers into our design choices. By preserving significant landmarks and engaging with the local community, we can breathe life into the translation, making it a living reflection of Allston's past, present, and future aspirations.

What is the land use code for the sounds of Allston's storied rock history? What is the FAR of the many histories of Brighton Park? How might these elements, which are necessarily excluded from conventional design processes for lack of methods and means, be incorporated into a total design for Allston, and how would this change the behaviors, perceptions, and urbanisms around this underappreciated neighborhood?

The dynamics of urban life transcend physical design, encompassing all of the narratives, events, and people that unfold within these physical designs. While we can envision plazas, parks, and public areas with conventional urban design, it typically does not encapsulate the richness of human experience that truly defines these spaces. In the case of a bustling market square, it is not just about the design of stalls and seating but also about the energy of traders hawking their goods and neighbors greeting each other with warmth and familiarity. In these instances, designers must strive to create environments that invite and nurture these vibrant social exchanges. And what more vibrant bit of planned inspiration might we find than that of the theme park?

Chapter 3

Theme Parks: An Alternative History of Urban Design

Michael Sorkin, in his provocatively titled edited volume *Variations on a Theme Park: The New American City and the End of Public Space*, argued that the "new city" is one of globalized mass culture, obsessive security, cocooning, and simulation.[1] His trenchant critique connected these trends, bemoaning a practice of urban design that is "almost wholly preoccupied with reproduction, with the creation of urbane disguises," harkening to Disneyland or perhaps the ersatz European appliqué in the décor of a shopping mall.[2] While the political and economic arguments Sorkin highlighted certainly ring ever truer in the hyper-gentrified city of our contemporary kleptocratic capitalism, his critique glosses over the design strategies and tactics offered through the examination of the theme park. These urban design practices are value-neutral in their own

1 Michael Sorkin, ed., *Variations on a Theme Park: The New American City and the End of Public Space* (New York: The Noonday Press, 1992).

2 Ibid., 14.

right, only descending into Sorkin's dark vision of the future in conjunction with the dehumanizing political and economic trends that commingle in the theme park of our contemporary minds: the profit-seeking, gated, and privatized spaces of theme parks in a capitalist society that steal cultural histories and flatten, homogenize, and package them for sale to consumers at exorbitant prices. What, though, of the actual urban design strategies used in theme parks for organizing space, celebrating culture, and providing collective experience? While these strategies can certainly be used for ill, they can also be dreamt of as tools in a utopian urban design toolkit where spatial organization, storytelling, and experience drive a sense of shared publicness, where we can connect in spaces that are for all rather than for the highest bidder.

While the contemporary theme park has become something of a specter in urban design discourse, as a stand-in for a "real" city, this chapter will present an alternative history of the theme park as a kind of history of urban design itself. We ought to learn from these spaces of collective play rather than dismiss them, and, indeed, they have only recently become so subsumed and synonymous with the perils of our contemporary capitalism. This chapter presents, in a way, the kind of "practical past" that Hayden White has described, delving into our childhood experiences at the theme park rather than the abstract and bookish histories we've read of modernity and urbanism.[3] Indeed, we can trace an alternative lineage of urban design outside of its typical modernist touchstones like Haussmann and CIAM, one that observes the evolution of the theme park as a primary driver in how we understand cities and their design. The predecessors of the theme park, like the pleasure garden, are also intertwined with the origins of landscape architecture, suggesting promise in informing how we organize and understand the spaces and places where we experience everyday life.

In this chapter, we will go down the rabbit hole of the theme park. On the other side, maybe we'll find a whole new world of possibility, one of shared dreaming, fantastic storytelling, and new strategies for urban design. We'll consider a history of theme parks by type, giving us a typology through which we can analyze their structuring elements. Namely, we will explore how theme parks are spatially organized by narrative and experience, giving us new tools for organizing the city through urban design. We will also explore the idea of place-embedded history as a driver of narrative creation, and finally conclude with a closer look at the media of the theme park. These media point toward some of the many tools that theme parks offer in our urban design tool kit—tools that, just maybe, you might use yourself as you imagine the city of tomorrow.

3 Hayden White, *The Practical Past* (Evanston: Northwestern University Press, 2014).

Theme Park as Type

Theme parks, more generally referred to as amusement parks, can trace their lineage back to the French and English gardens that would later provide the disciplinary content for landscape architecture. They also share DNA with world fairs and expositions, which laid the groundwork for much of urban design, particularly within the American context (e.g., the World's Columbian Exposition which set the stage for the City Beautiful movement), as well as served to further a variety of architectural exploits (e.g., Le Corbusier's early lambasting of then-conventional architecture with his Pavillon de l'Esprit Nouveau at the Paris Exposition des Arts Décoratifs of 1925). Theme parks, however, were not canonized into cultural production—let alone high cultural production—disciplinary tradition, or even professionalization in the same way. For reasons largely linked to their "low" cultural standing, theme parks have remained a poorly understood and understudied form from spatial, design, and cultural perspectives. Even those designers and firms which focus on the design of themed spaces tend to be somewhat isolated from the broader cultural flows and social networks of conventionally understood architecture and urban design practice.

In the same way that Frederick Law Olmsted and Daniel Burnham drew from English gardens and world fairs, respectively, to produce a particular type of urbanism, so too might theme parks serve as a conceptual model for another type of urbanism. Over the course of their historical development, they have gone through many variations but have maintained particular typological constants that suggest structures for urbanism. Specifically, theme parks have always maintained comprehensive, networked mediatic structures that guide experience within a space of destinations. The "destinations" are less important, ranging from roller coasters to restaurants, their primary relationship to the overall structure of a theme park is to dictate the size of the crowd that will remain in proximity to their adjacent space. They are the equivalent of interior private spaces within a city; an urban designer only needs to know the exterior quality and the number of people and things that will reside within, or enter and exit, that space. Rather, the visual and experiential indicators within the shared space of the theme park—the space between the destinations—are the proto-urban structure from which we can learn.

Scan of plan for Vauxhall Gardens by Thomas Allen, 1826. Source: author. Allen includes this legend in a book titled Parish of Lambeth (J. Nichols, 1826), in the spelling of his time: "1. Fire work Tower; 2. Evening Star; 3. Hermitage; 4. Smugglers Cave; 5. House in which M. Barrett died; 6. Statue of Milton; 7. Transparency; 8. Theatre; 9. Chinese entrance; 10. Artificers work shops; 11. Octagon temples; 12. Fountain; 13. Circles of Boxes; 14. Orchestra; 15. Collonade; 16. Rotunda; 17. Picture Room; 18. Supper Room; 19. Ice House; 20. Bar; 21. Princes Pavillion; 22. Entrance; 23. Water Gate; 24. House."

Pleasure Garden: Vauxhall Gardens

Vauxhall Gardens in London became one of the first internationally recognized theme parks, then known as "pleasure gardens," after it opened in 1661. In France, pleasure gardens began as an outgrowth of traditional gardens, but in England, they often began as an outgrowth of an inn or tavern. Incorporating visceral pleasures into the otherwise pristine garden, pleasure gardens generally included circus acts, music, dancing, food, and drink, platted in relation to each other and to the garden's plantings, providing a set of queer spaces where titillating and subversive activities could be performed in a semi-public space apart from the everyday reality of then-puritanical England.

Amusement Park: Steeplechase Park

Steeplechase Park can be identified as the clearest prototype of the American theme park. Officially opened in 1897 by the so-called "king of the American amusement park," George Cornelius Tilyou, Steeplechase Park developed over a long period, beginning with Tilyou's parents setting up a hotel on Coney Island, to their building the island's first theater, to his importing of one of the world's first Ferris wheels after he saw the noted first deployed at the Chicago World's Fair.[4] Consolidating these developments around another new experience, "The Steeplechase Ride," or an early form of a roller coaster, Tilyou began charging admission to the overall park and allowing free use of the amusements once inside. Tilyou also began the practice of searching around the world for new attractions that could be added to the park, constantly changing the organization and form of its plan. Such dynamism allowed Steeplechase to outlast its bigger and more lavish derivatives on Coney Island, Luna Park and Dreamland. Later, Rem Koolhaas would describe the developments on Coney Island as prototypical for a form of delirious urbanism, a congested Manhattanism:

> *To survive as a resort—a place offering contrast—Coney Island is thus forced to mutate: it must turn itself into a total opposite of Nature, it has no choice but to counteract the artificiality of the new metropolis with its own Super-Natural. Instead of suspension of urban pressure, it offers intensification. Even the most intimate aspects of human nature are subjected to experiment on. If life in the metropolis creates loneliness and alienation, Coney Island counterattacks this with the Barrels of Love. Two horizontal cylinders—mounted in line—revolve slowly in opposite directions. At either end, a small staircase leads up to an entrance. One feeds men into the machine, the other women. It is impossible to remain standing. Men and women fall on top of each other. The unrelenting rotation of the machine fabricates synthetic intimacy between people who would never otherwise have met...*[5]

4 Gary Kyriazi, *The Great American Amusement Parks* (Secaucus: Citadel Press, 1976), 42.

5 Rem Koolhaas, *Delirious New York: A Retroactive Manifesto for Manhattan* (New York: The Monacelli Press, 1997).

Entrance to Steeplechase Park. Photograph by Detroit Publishing Co., 1903.
Source: Library of Congress, LC-D4-16697.

Aerial view of Pacific Ocean Park in Santa Monica, California from a postcard published by Mitock & Sons, c. 1959.
Source: Wikimedia Commons.

Amusement Pier: Pacific Park

In a sense, all of Coney Island could be considered a form of amusement pier as it was organized with the beach. Amusement piers generally occur either along an ocean-front boardwalk or on an actual pier that extends into the ocean. The various incarnations of Pacific Park near Santa Monica and Venice in Southern California typify this form of theme park, including the original Ocean Park Pier that opened in 1926 and closed in 1956, the reincarnation of Ocean Park as Pacific Ocean Park which was designed to compete with Disneyland and was open from 1958 to 1967, and its current Pacific Park version on the Santa Monica Pier that opened in 1996. While Pacific Park nods to the earlier Pacific Ocean Park, it is located on a different pier as the original pier was subject to arson and was ultimately demolished by 1975, leaving only a few underwater piles. Organized in a highly compressed, linear fashion, amusement piers owe their form to the surrounding ocean and the spatial and structural capacities of the pier.

Trolley Park: Idora Park

The Lagoon at Idora Park, Youngstown, Ohio from a postcard published by Charles D. Hoover, c. 1918. Source: The Gayraj.

While theme parks, as a microcosm of their surroundings, contain transportation elements within themselves, trolley parks were intentionally planned in conjunction with the expansion of urban streetcar lines to attract riders to their terminuses. Urban rail, at this time, was typically a private enterprise as well, providing economic synergies between profits made from ridership and from attendance at trolley parks. Idora Park, in Youngstown, Ohio, was one such park; indeed, it was originally named "Terminus Park" and included free admission with the purchase of trolley fare, as it opened in 1899. Highly successful until the dominant form of transportation in the US transitioned from urban rail lines to the automobile, Idora Park lasted to the '80s because its open plan allowed for changing patterns of use, even though it was constrained on its 27 acres of space—at its end, it was largely used for church and company picnics. It ultimately closed in 1984 after a fire destroyed its biggest attractions, and was purchased by the Mt. Calvary Pentecostal Church to become something of a religious theme park called "The City of God." The church was never able to make good on its vision and a series of fires reduced the property to vacant space. Today, it remains vacant as the church is embroiled in tax and bankruptcy issues.

Factory Tour Garden: Hersheypark

View of Hersheypark from its botanical garden, 2019. Photograph by Carol M. Highsmith. Source: Library of Congress, LC-DIG-highsm-58109.

Hersheypark relied on its own historical and social cache as a global chocolate producer rather than thrills and shows as "destinations" within its organization. After a tour of the factory, visitors could spend a relaxing afternoon in the park with rides, pools, and shows of a decidedly less flashy nature than their counterparts in other parks. Started as a place of relaxation for company employees, the factory tour garden opened in 1905 and continues to operate to this day. Hersheypark operated on these terms, slowly incorporating more conventional amusement park rides until its renovation, expansion, and theming in 1970 after the huge crowds could no longer fit into the factory, transforming the tranquil park into a hyperreal version of Hershey, typified by an entire land called Chocolate World with attractions such as "The Really Big 3-D Show" featuring John O'Hurley and Danny DeVito. This success would soon be imitated by Anheuser-Busch in their still-operating chain of Busch Gardens.

Thrill Park: Six Flags Over Texas

Scan of "Outlaws bite the dust" postcard featuring the "Texas Section" of Six Flags Over Texas, c. 1961. Source: author.

The first instance of the now ubiquitous Six Flags chain was Six Flags Over Texas, opened in 1961 by Angus Wynne. A paean to Texas, the park is themed by historical periods in the state's development. While all theme parks use thrill rides, the thrill park is unique in that it is a proto-form of the theme park typified by Disneyland with separate themed zones and an overall layout and design that maximizes crowd dispersion and consumption—though here the rides are of the same variety as past amusement parks (roller coasters and so on) with a limited set of media that define these themes. These are largely low-capital media, including signage and names, as well as music and particular performances, such as a "Western hootenanny" in the "Republic of Texas" themed area.[6]

6 Kyriazi, *The Great American Amusement Parks*, 185.

Theme Park: Disneyland

Disneyland, even more so than Six Flags, is the theme park par excellence. Since its wild expense and formula-defying content (there were to be no typical amusement park rides) were unleashed in 1955, every park has since tried to emulate its success. It was the first to truly utilize theming (I generously use the term "theme park" to refer to its precursors as well) and Walt Disney was relentless in ensuring that every element of each area was uniform and highly structured, from the employee uniforms to the signage and ambient music. Like Tilyou's original park, it was never declared finished, and each year new attractions and whole themed areas, or "lands," were added. Perhaps most significantly, Disneyland was able to draw from its own cultural and mediatic lore, linking rides and beloved Disney characters, as well as linking Disneyland to a successful TV show on ABC, which, incidentally, was started out of a need for raising additional construction funding.

Disney, in fact, uses many traditional urban planning and design strategies in the layout of their parks, including axial layout patterns and particular attention to networks (primarily pedestrian paths), nodes (such as key rides or central areas of a particular "land"), and figure-ground analysis of areas that are visible and accessible to "guests" and those that are "back of house." Their parks also rely on a variety of narrative and place-based theming strategies: agglomerations of parks will typically have one of a "Magic Kingdom" park based on traditional Disney rides and intellectual property, a place-based park based on real-world contexts such as California Adventure, and a "studio backlot" style park such as "Hollywood Studios" in Orlando's Disney World. There are also a handful of other types, such as animal or water themed parks. In our current era of Disney dominance, as they have vacuumed up more and more intellectual property from brands like Lucasfilms and Marvel Comics, there has emerged a high degree of interlocking symbiosis between the company's IP and its parks. Where once you might have a theme park ride that had nothing to do with creative IP, or a successful series of animated films like the *Cars* movies from Pixar, now for these elements to exist independently is a near impossibility. We are on the slow march for every ride to have a film and, conversely, every film to have a ride. Indeed, Disney films now are often scripted and shot with key scenes that are intentionally created to translate nicely into a theme park ride.

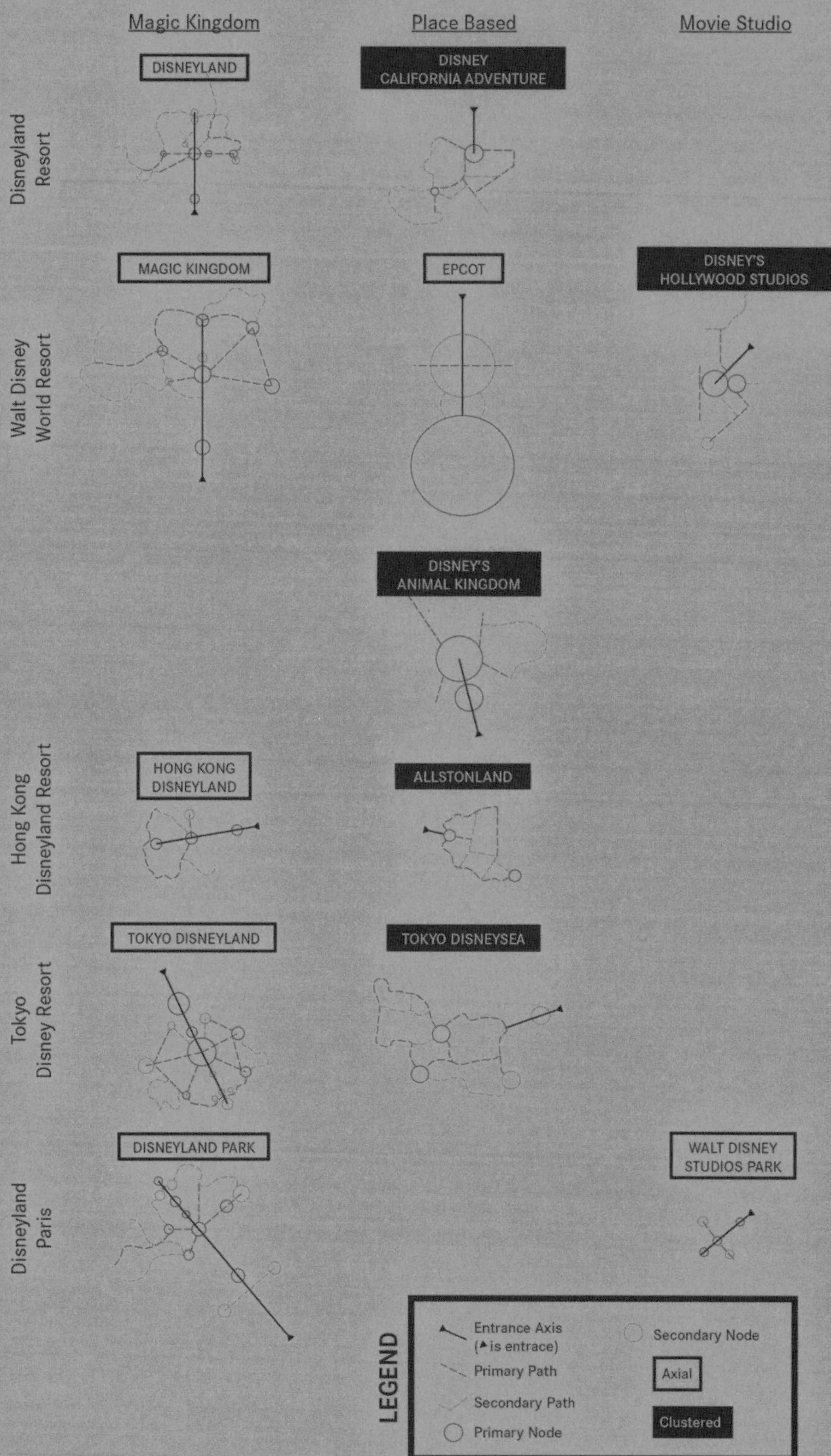

Organizational patterns in Disney parks and the imagined Allstonland. Source: author.

Misunderstanding Scripted Space

Some of the most cunning users of media in space turn out to be designers for retail or so-called "experience architecture." Designers of, say, themed housing developments or a new shopping mall tend to have a very keen awareness of how various media operate in space, affecting bodies—usually shoppers—within that space. One such example is the now defunct Hollister flagship store in the SoHo neighborhood of New York City, designed in 2010 by Meyers + Associates. The experience goes something like this. One passes into a nondescript building between two shirtless, muscular men who are staked out on Broadway. You discover a darkened, cavernous space with pulsating music and the scent of cologne drifting about. Employees—all attractive and tan—have been instructed to ask you a Californian "What's up" with a wink as you pass by, elevating your ego as though you could be their friend in real life. You ascend staircase after staircase and can see huge, mullioned plasma screens that live-simulcast California beaches, making one think that you have been transported out of the hard, old East Coast into a laid-back and titillating world of sand and sun; you are in another world. One can't help but purchase a sweater or two![7]

7 It can also drive you to violence or evacuation in two other publicized instances. And the store has since closed because of repeated issues with bedbugs and other vermin.

Norman Klein refers to this adept use of media as "scripted space," a decidedly clinical term for what is generally referred to as theming.[8] The other famous example, of course, is Walt Disney's Disneyland. Spawned into numerous parks around the world, they are the quintessential example for a deliberate and complete control of media as environments to provide a sensorial escape for their "guests." Scripted space is space that has been intentionally designed with respect to how one moves through it, how narrative unfolds spatially, and how we perceive established signs and symbols that aggregate to a coherent and convincing whole despite however far-fetched it all might seem once you pass the space's thresholds.

8 Norman Klein, *The Vatican to Vegas: A History of Special Effects* (New York: New Press, 2004).

Too often, the techniques and tools of scripted space are thrown out as invalid, misunderstood, and conflated with the currents of neoliberal capital. But one cannot ignore the widespread popularity of such spaces; whatever their motives, they connect with people on a visceral level—they work. Furthermore, scripted spaces are one of the precious few mechanisms that exist to embed meaning and identity into a generic world that has become immune to the injections of iconicity which provided a degree of relief in the pre-recession and pre-pandemic boom years of the '90s and aughts (consider, for example, the typical example of the Guggenheim Bilbao, now tired as a trope).

What if their effects were used toward public ends, rather than for profit? This is not a novel idea: one might argue that scripted space has existed, and with *civitas* in mind, for as long as antiquity. The classical orders hold all the necessary traits of a themed space. As do cathedrals and their ecclesiastical floorplans. There is a defined set of signs and symbols that are internally consistent and would be understood by the people in and around them. This structure is used to provide meaning and value—just that it happens to be a set of ideal forms reflecting the divine rather than a set of traditional Main Street façades that reflect Americana as one would find in Disneyland's Main Street, U.S.A.

Narratives of the Spellbound Story World

Every facet of these parks, from their surroundings to their structures and layouts, intertwine to create an immersive and memorable thematic experience. The underlying objective is to present a cohesive narrative, akin to a storyboard brought to life through architectural, spatial, and urban design, thereby captivating the visitors with an unforgettable tale.

From the start, the narrative is considered essential. Storytelling is used as a strategy to structure the visitors' journey, stage their experiences, and market destinations.[9] Also, co-creation is now commonly used in tourism, in which narrative is a conduit for the participatory creation of experience. Scholars have noted that tourist attractions, such as theme parks, have narratives to provide a memorable experience for visitors; theme parks have a "concrete narrative intention" through the presentation of narrative architecture in its physical space.[10] Narrative and storytelling, long the domain of the humanities, turns out to be a critical component for urban design practice, and one that ought to be integrated more into design pedagogy.

9 Johan R. Edelheim. *Tourist Attractions: From Object to Narrative* (Bristol: Channel View Publications, 2016).

10 Salvador Anton Clavé, *The Global Theme Park Industry* (Wallingford: CABI, 2011).

The main objective of using narrative architecture in theme park design is to create a story world, in which all rides are stand-alone channels for narrative information. Some 77 major theme parks in Europe, Asia, and North America were analyzed with respect to these practices, and it was determined that narrative, such as explicit storytelling, narrative rides, themed rides, and so on, were a critical architectural design component.[11] The findings revealed that 89% of these parks follow a discernible theme, showing the dominance of this approach pioneered with Disneyland. While narrative theory is primarily associated with humanities scholarship, its allure extends to theme park design, where it shapes the very attractions that beckon visitors. Narratives permeate all tourist attractions, infusing theme parks in particular with multiple texts that narrate a captivating story to visitors. In essence, theme parks adopt narrative design to elucidate how their physical spaces shall be "experienced and understood" by their guests.[12]

The process, one that could be used by any urban designer working on an urban plan, involves a combination of careful attention toward existing narratives in space and the intentional deployment of these and newly constructed narratives that are connected to specific spaces and places. It isn't so different than many design practices that begin with a bit of research and continue on to drawing—though in this case, sketches and drawings take the form of a storyboard, mapping out how a narrative flows over time and through space, contending with how inhabitants move through a space and experience particular urban moments in sequences over time.

11 Carissa Baker, "The Prevalence of Storyworlds and Thematic Landscapes in Global Theme Parks," *Annals of Tourism Research Empirical Insights* 4, no. 1 (2023): 1-10, https://doi.org/10.1016/j.annale.2022.100080.

12 Edelheim, *Tourist Attractions*, 112.

Crafting Enchanting Public Spaces

In recent years, the themed entertainment market has skyrocketed, becoming a major force in marketing and economics worldwide. According to recent estimations, the global theme park market is projected to reach a staggering increase of $82.4 billion USD by 2030, underscoring its continued popularity.[13] Where designers have looked askance at theme parks and theming, the appetite for their offerings by your average person has only continued to grow. These spaces offer myriad possibilities for entertainment, dining, relaxation, excitement, spending time with friends and loved ones, and perhaps most of all, a moment of respite from the monotony of work in a capitalist society, a brief time of escape form the psychological pressure of living through the Anthropocene with its multiple and intersecting crises and catastrophes.

Central to the allure of theme parks is the art of theming itself, a craft that weaves together visitors' emotions, images of

13 Global Industry Analysts, Inc., *Amusement and Theme Parks: A Global Strategic Business Report* (San Jose: Global Industry Analysts, Inc., 2023).

distinct times and places, and underlying messages into a spatial tapestry. According to Lukas, theming is mainly used to "symbolically and conceptually organize a space," in which a theme plays a significant role in attracting visitors to parks through the specificity and accessibility of such symbols—and there is no reason why a similar strategy couldn't be used in creating urban designs for cities.[14] Theming takes common culture and transforms it into space and place. Without the narrative ubiquity of Disney and all its intellectual property, Disneyland certainly wouldn't be such a success, cashing in on our collective nostalgia or shared cultural narratives.

But there are a wealth of narratives, signs, and symbols that operate outside of the closed off walls of intellectual property—just think of the whirlwind creative and cultural production found within internet memes. Who could possibly claim to own a meme, the flash in the pan of NFTs aside. Far from arguing for the meme-ification of public space, I instead suggest that we ought to stake a public claim in our culture and use that culture for the better design of our shared urban spaces. As Lukas suggests, a big part of the allure of themed spaces isn't only for their understood cultural symbols but, rather, that they cohere a space that is comforting, that makes sense, and that is symbolically and conceptually organized. In our current day of chaos and disaster, we simply want to exist for a moment in a place that makes a bit of sense.

Envision, then, a city park that unfolds like a mesmerizing tale, guiding visitors through curated landscapes and interactive marvels, stoking emotions and curiosity alike. Picture a public plaza transformed into a living stage, with moving performances, themed events, and captivating art installations, transforming the space into a thriving, dynamic hub for the community to congregate and recreate. In the nexus of theme park design and urban planning lies an enticing opportunity: the crafting of enchanting and inclusive urban environments that elicit joy, inspiration, and a profound sense of community.

How does one accomplish all this? Beyond careful attention to narrative, the urban designer must become a master of signs and symbols that exist within the cultural landscape and consider how to translate these signs and symbols into material and spatial form. Theme parks serve as nodes in transmedia storytelling, stretching across video games, television shows, movies, books, and even fan activities. Williams aptly coins the term "spatial transmedia" or "drillable immersion" to describe theme parks, as they seamlessly meld different geographies, cultures, and narratives into a harmonious whole.[15] As a result, theme parks achieve their narrative aspirations through meticulous design, fostering living scenes and immersive environments that envelop visitors in spellbinding experiences. Let's take, for example, our humble neighborhood of Allston as a case in point once again.

14 Scott A. Lukas, *The Immersive Worlds Handbook: Designing Theme Parks and Consumer Spaces* (London: Routledge, 2019).

15 Rebecca Williams, *Theme Park Fandom: Spatial Transmedia, Materiality and Participatory Cultures* (Amsterdam: Amsterdam University Press, 2020).

Displacement: Allstonland in Hong Kong

Chapter 4

Let us consider a form of approximate translation: displacement. Displacement has at its heart the same mechanism that Bertolt Brecht called the "V-Effect" or "alienation effect" in his theory of epic theater, but which might as easily be called cognitive shock.[1] Rather than bother with the suspension of disbelief or even the maintenance of the fourth wall, Brecht believed in brute force. A variety of techniques were employed to continuously remind the audience that they were actively watching a play rather than passively losing themselves in fantasy. Actors would obviously play multiple characters, or internal thought processes would unnaturally be voiced, acting like shock therapy for the mind.

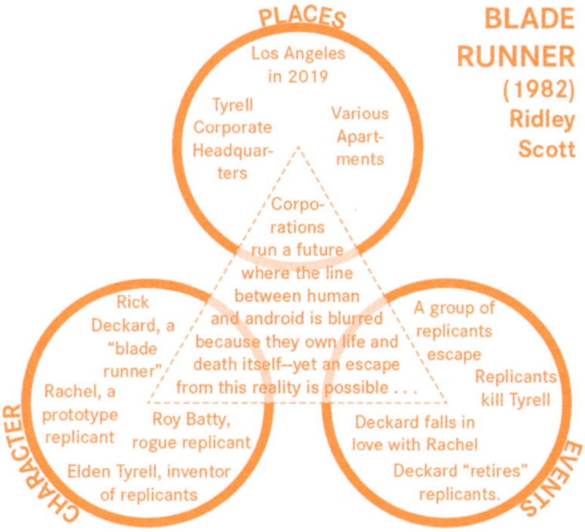

The essential character-event-place triptych of narrative. Source: author.

1 Bertold Brecht, "Alienation Effects in Chinese Acting," in *Brecht on Theater: The Development of an Aesthetic*, ed. John Willett (New York: Hill and Wang, 1964 [essay first published in 1936]), 91–99.

In the same way, the act of translating a neighborhood like Allston into a theme park in Hong Kong—let's call it "Allstonland"—serves to distance the "audience" from any assumed reality in Allston, while simultaneously preventing a passive consumption of Allstonland-as-reality in Hong Kong. When this fine line between the assumption of reality and consumption of the imaginary is pulled taut, several benefits emerge. While Allston is a shabby and shunned neighborhood, its ideal reconstruction in Hong Kong provides for social uplift through its demonstration of what Allston could be; yet, at the same time, it remains only a demonstration and not a replacement for the real thing. Breaking Allston's content out of the fourth wall compels us to realize its constructed nature and more actively participate in its production. Allstonland provides a controlled testing ground for scenarios that might be risky or impractical in real space, yet still require the rigor of thinking through the implications of design, like a kind of large-scale architectural model.

While displacement can occur through media structured in ways apart from the theme park, theme parks nevertheless offer a particularly useful means of analysis because of how events play out within scripted space. As it turns out, similar event scripting is playing an ever-larger role in urban spaces. As urbanist Dennis Frenchman has described, places have become inextricably linked to the events that unfold within them (e.g., Providence's "WaterFire"), providing not only a unique identity but also a trajectory toward directed social and physical development.[2] And, indeed, as Allston is displaced into Allstonland, the events that already unfold within its boundaries become evident as catalysts that can transform it from a space in which particular events "happen to happen" to an event-place where these particular events are fundamentally linked to the identity, development, and value of Allston as a place.

We can unpack and analyze the process of displacement through the consideration of the essential elements of film narratives. We can break any movie down into three components: characters, be they human or non-human, with psychological profiles that drive intent or lack thereof; events, actions undertaken by or done to the characters, or broader event-contexts in which these characters exist; and places, where these characters are and where these events happen. If we take Ridley Scott's *Blade Runner*, for example, we see a narrative unfold based on the intersection of Deckard (a character) seeking to "retire" (an event) a group of replicants (more characters) who flee from him (another event) from apartments in a dilapidated part of town (a place) to Tyrell's (yet another character) headquarters (another place) in a future dystopian Los Angeles (a place that contains these other places) where corporations rule (an event-context).

You can break all kinds of texts, be they literary or cinematic, down to this triptych, though the filmic medium lays these elements particularly bare because of its visual and time-based nature. Together, they create a narrative, the essence of being in this world. But without any one of these elements, the others lose a sense of meaning, of identity. This is especially true for place, the most often overlooked leg of this stool. The fundamental idea of displacement is that by moving characters and events from one place to another, you truly begin to see cracks begin to form, you begin to understand what makes these characters and events particular, and the rest falls away.

2 Dennis Frenchman, "Event-Places in North America: City Meaning and Making," *Places* 16, no. 3 (2004): 36–49.

Translating displacement as defined in the domain of physics—a vector quantity representing both magnitude and direction—to the context of urban design holds a similar multidimensional significance. The concept of displacement in city planning and development extends beyond mere physical movement; it encompasses the immensity or magnitude of psychological and emotional transformations that occur when individuals and communities are uprooted and relocated to new environments. This notion of displacement as a vector quantity provides a lens through which we can understand the intricate dynamics of urban spaces and the effects their change can have on the human mind.

As we venture into new territories, the brain undergoes a remarkable process of adaptation, learning, and relearning to cope with the shifting nature of information that it is processing. Research has shown how visual relocation can serve as an instructional tool: in one study, for example, prismatic displacement enhanced participants' spatial comprehension.[3] Such findings suggest that exposing ourselves to diverse environments can enrich our cognitive abilities, much like the brain's ability to adapt to multiple and even dramatic changes simultaneously, highlighting its extraordinary capacity for learning and adaptation.

Another dimension of displacement is connected to our brain's ability to tap into the subconscious: scholars have demonstrated that many of our behaviors originate from unconscious decisions made in reaction to environmental factors.[4] Displacement can act as a form of signaling, introducing people to unfamiliar stimuli which prompt the brain to move from unconscious to conscious intention, catalyzing interactions with one's surroundings in novel ways. In this sense, displacement can contribute to the development of metacognitive abilities, enabling higher order processes like adaptation, recognition, and discrimination.[5] Similarly, others have noted that particular systems of the subconscious mind, including the perceptual systems that govern our spatial abilities, may not be counterpoints to our "real" conscious mind but actually completely independent systems that simply do not feed into our conscious, reflective, and metacognitive mental systems without a bit of an intentional shock, such as displacement.[6]

All of this is of particular interest for urban designers because of the relationship and differences between how an urban designer analyzes and intervenes in space versus how a user of that space interacts with it. Where urban designers can inject these unconscious signals into plans for a space, improving it for its users, designers must consciously and even meta-consciously engage with a space to shape and design it with intention. Displacement can do precisely that, allowing the signals from our unconscious perceptual systems to travel into our conscious mind.

3 Gordon M. Redding and Benjamin Wallace, "Adaptive Spatial Alignment and Strategic Perceptual-Motor Control," *Journal of Experimental Psychology: Human Perception and Performance* 22, no. 2 (1996): 379–94, https://doi.org/10.1037/0096-1523.22.2.379.

4 Ruud Custers and Henk Aarts, "The Unconscious Will: How the Pursuit of Goals Operates outside of Conscious Awareness," *Science* 329, no. 5987 (2010): 47–50, https://doi.org/10.1126/science.1188595.

5 Athanasios Drigas and Eleni Mitsea, "The 8 Pillars of Metacognition," *International Journal of Emerging Technologies in Learning (iJET)* 15, no. 21 (2020): 162–178, https://doi.org/10.3991/ijet.v15i21.14907. See also: Peter Carruthers, *The Opacity of Mind: An Integrative Theory of Self-Knowledge* (Oxford: Oxford University Press, 2011); Joëlle Proust, *The Philosophy of Metacognition: Mental Agency and Self-Awareness* (Oxford: Oxford University Press, 2013).

6 John A. Bargh and Ezequiel Morsella, "The Unconscious Mind," *Perspectives on Psychological Science* 3, no. 1 (2008): 73–79, https://doi.org/10.1111/j.1745-6916.2008.00064.x.

A Shklovskian Perspective

The notion of defamiliarization, as coined by Russian literary theorist Viktor Shklovsky, provides another lens through which we can understand displacement and the experience of venturing into new places. Shklovsky describes Tolstoy as "defamiliarizing" the idea of flogging in the short story "Shame" by describing it with unfamiliar language rather than using more familiar and accepted language.[7] By describing a scene with actions like "to strip people," "to hurl them to the floor," and "to lash about on the naked buttocks," he shocks the reader into awareness of what might otherwise be noted with anodyne language: the criminal was sentenced to flogging.

Shklovsky notes that this is a common technique in literature, "found almost everywhere form is found," and we can easily use this technique in all other sorts of media as well—not least of all, the urban plan.[8] Urban planners can learn from the tool of displacement to create spaces where people are offered an alternative to the comfortable familiar. By compelling ourselves to adapt to new environments, enabling the sympathetic nervous system and heightening perception and awareness, we are forced to gain a deeper understanding of our spatial surroundings, unveiling hidden dimensions of the urban landscape. Displacement can enable analysis of what Bill Hillier has called space syntax: the spatial configurations of our built environment, along with the flows, human interactions, and uses that occur within it.[9]

7 Viktor Shklovsky, "Art as Technique," in *Russian Formalist Criticism: Four Essays* (Lincoln: University of Nebraska Press, 1917), 3–24.

8 Ibid.

9 Bill Hillier, *Space Is the Machine: A Configurational Theory of Architecture* (London: Space Syntax, 1996).

All of this to say, defamiliarization can be a powerful practice which aids urban designers in the process of shaping places using otherwise conventional urban design principles—considerations such as aesthetics, scale, texture, color, material, sustainability, governance, participation, and so on.[10] Of course, it is important for the urban designer to remember to "refamiliarize" a space at times: overuse of displacement can sometimes disrupt people's sense of community and belonging, leaving them feeling disconnected and isolated.[11] Similarly, defamiliarization can evoke feelings of alienation and estrangement as the familiar is rendered unfamiliar.[12] Displacement is for a cognitive shock, something valuable to a professional designer, but to be used intentionally, cautiously, and sparingly for designs that are to be consumed by the public. Here, though, I must also cite Homi Bhabha who writes, citing Fredric Jameson, that displacement is actually necessary for a process of uncovering the unrepresentable pathways of global capital, and for outlining the contours of culture within this topology (so, perhaps, we ought to use displacement in a not-so-cautious way from time to time):

> *It is, ironically, the disintegrative moment, even movement, of enunciation—that sudden disjunction of the present—that makes possible the rendering of culture's global reach. And, paradoxically, it is only through a structure of splitting and displacement—"the fragmented and schizophrenic decentering of the self"—that the architecture of the new historical subject emerges at the limits of representation itself, "to enable a situational representation on the part of the individual to that vaster and unrepresentable totality which is the ensemble of society's structures as a whole."*[13]

10 Matthew Carmona, *Public Places Urban Spaces: The Dimensions of Urban Design* (London: Routledge, 2010).

11 John Douglas Porteous, "Home: The Territorial Core," *Geographical Review* 66, no. 4 (1976): 383–390, https://doi.org/10.2307/213649.

12 Shklovsky, "Art as Technique," 5.

13 Homi Bhabha, *The Location of Culture* (London: Routledge, 2004 [1994]), 310.

When delving into the realm of urban planning and development, displacement is more than a symbolic gesture, important as that may be. Displacement also encapsulates the profound psychological and emotional transformations that individuals and communities undergo when they are compelled to contend with changes to their environment, or even moreso, to uproot and settle in a new environment. But these transformations need not be from a physical or permanent move to a new home: lesser permanent and negative versions can be triggered from travel for leisure, immersing oneself in a fantastical movie, or even embarking on a journey to a theme park, enabling learning and delight. It is critical to distinguish the potentials and impacts of the conceptual design strategy of displacement from the positive effects of temporary displacement and, most of all, the deeply troubling issue of unwanted and permanent displacement experienced by people experiencing gentrification, poverty, homelessness, war, and the like.

The potential embedded in the positive version of displacement is this: the act of traversing from one place to another grants us a more profound understanding of our position in time and space and forces us to contend with the everyday realities that we may take for granted or perhaps not even notice at all. My aim in this chapter is to explore how such displacement can be utilized as an urban design technique, transforming our assumptions about a project or site, altering our perspectives, broadening our horizons, and breaking us out of our habits and expectations.

As for Allston, we'll test out the urban design strategy of displacement by pulling out the basic elements of the site—its formal properties like massing, its programmatic qualities such as its land use, and its place-embedded histories—and placing them in a totally different context. And, for good measure, we'll translate them from real spaces to imagined ones: Allston will become a theme park. Hong Kong is as good a place as any for this imaginary proposal, and it has the benefit of being home to one of the Disneyland theme parks located around the globe. Borrowing from this new destination, we'll learn from Hong Kong's urbanism, its Hong Kong Disneyland theme park planning and design, and all that displacement has to offer. We will create Allstonland, the Hong Kong theme park based on Allston that you never knew you wanted—or, for that matter, imagined was even possible!

A Labyrinthine Metropolis

Hong Kong stands as a fascinating case study for urban researchers, courtesy of its distinctive urban layout and sociopolitical context. The city's landscape, with its towering buildings, narrow streets, and unexpected urban spatialities, such as elevated walkways and underground corridors replacing the conventional street grid, never fails to surprise first-time visitors. Yet at the same time, this dense metropolis is also known for its interconnection with the surrounding natural environment, with residents having a high degree of ecological awareness.[14]

However, Hong Kong's layout comes with its own challenges for its inhabitants. The complexities of moving within the city can be daunting, and issues like unaffordable housing costs and gentrification are further exacerbated by rapid population growth against an already very high density.[15] This underscores the urgency for urban planning strategies that consider the cultural and social ramifications of urban change. How might Hong Kong teach us urban lessons for Allston?

14 Rebecca L. H. Chiu, "Socio-Cultural Sustainability of Housing: A Conceptual Exploration," *Housing, Theory and Society* 21, no. 2 (2004): 65–76, https://doi.org/10.1080/14036090410014999.

15 Tai-Lok Lui, "Beneath the Appearance of Gentrification: Probing Local Complexities," *International Journal of Urban and Regional Research* 41, no. 3 (2017): 478–486, https://doi.org/10.1111/1468-2427.12497.

Hong Kong Disneyland and its curiously displaced identity within the skyline of Hong Kong. Source: author.

Hong Kong Disneyland, nestled on Penny's Bay on Lantau Island, stands as a captivating case study in urban design, but it comes with its own complex set of implications. While the magic of Disney's classic American theme park aesthetic remains at its core, the park's layout also purportedly incorporates *feng shui* principles and elements of Chinese culture, rendering it a sort of architectural fusion.[16] Penny's Bay is itself constructed from a fantasy: a port for hundreds of years, it was filled in and is no longer a bay but a peninsula, materialized from nothing to create land ready for Disneyland's original construction.

The theme park, like most, employs spatial displacement as a powerful tool to transport guests to an entirely different realm. Stepping onto Main Street, U.S.A., visitors find themselves whisked away to a picturesque American street from the early 20th century, surrounded by old time architecture and vintage automobiles, carefully crafted to elicit a sense of nostalgia and wonder.[17] This use of displacement, rather than cognitive shock, provides something like the opposite for many: guests enjoy an immersive and enchanting experience that lingers in their memories—perhaps giving a moment of reprieve from day-to-day life in one of the densest cities on the planet.

Yet for others, the cultural chasm between Hong Kong at large and this collection of Americana-themed sites may evoke feelings of unease or disconnect, a kind of soft power colonialism of the 21st century. Striking a balance between enchantment and consideration of cultural sensitivities is crucial for the park's appeal to a diverse audience; and, indeed, similar lessons ought to be absorbed by urban designers working in spaces outside the walls of the theme park.

16 Wing Yee Kimburley Choi, "Remade in Hong Kong: How Hong Kong People Use Hong Kong Disneyland" (PhD thesis, Lingnan University, 2007), https://doi.org/10.14793/cs_etd.6.

17 Ibid.

Power
Station
Inspiration
Lake
Additional
Parking
Parking and
Transit
Phase IIB
Expansion
Phase IIA Expansion
(Allstonland)
Existing
Disneyland
Park
Additional
Resort
Locations

From Allston to Allstonland

So let's get down to business. Here we are presented with the next opportunity for an act of approximate translation, an urban design strategy of displacement. To continue our example, let's start with our new, improved urban design for Allston. We have a fairly typical American neighborhood in an urban context, and we've improved its urban plan by better connecting its networks and sensibly filling in its urban form through figure-ground analysis. But let's go a little further. What might we learn from Hong Kong and, indeed, from the mental exercise of displacement to improve upon our designs for humble Allston? What would happen if we took the essence of Allston's urbanism—its urban syntax and its cultural content—and translated it into a theme park? And, moreover, what if we considered the implications of displacement, designing an Allston-based theme park located in Hong Kong? A mental exercise like this is a terrific approach for urban designers to shake themselves free of their assumptions, biases, and unconscious designerly routines—a cognitive shock to the system.

Due to a drawn-out political battle, a large, primed swath of land sits vacant just across Hong Kong Disneyland, waiting to be developed. Disney retained the right to develop this land for nearly a decade, though the land was turned into temporary COVID-19 facilities from 2020-23, and Disney's right to the space has since not been renewed. As a site for our thought experiment, it is perfect: it is on the opposite side of the planet from Allston, semi-tabula rasa, and ensconced in a themed media environment. The absurdity of this thought experiment is such that we can, just maybe, suspend disbelief. Allstonland, located in Hong Kong, the product of an act of displacement, a theme park based on the cultural material of Allston. This process requires a degree of earnest respect, and we can afford it, because the project is strangely plausible.

Opposite page: Site plan for Hong Kong Disneyland and its neighboring vacant land, ready for Allstonland. Source: author.

Our first step is to isolate the various strands of experience that one might have in Allston. To transform them into rides, restaurants, and experiences within our theme park is to understand them on their terms in a way that is preposterous in their original contexts. And here is the key to approximate translation: we don't provide a one-to-one relocation of, say, Paradise Rock Club from Allston onto the reclaimed land of Penny's Bay. Rather, its approximate translation and conjoining with Brighton Music Hall into Paradise Music Hall allow us to perceive its possible alternate realities while maintaining its core DNA and its relationships to its spatial and spiritual adjacencies. Or the former CSX Railyard becomes an excavation of the very idea of the palimpsest of the city, transformed into the CSX Excavation ride in Brighton Park land where one rides through submerged layers of history. Approximate translation abstracts the real enough to enable critical analysis on spatial, actor-

Plan and rendering for the CSX Excavation ride in the Brighton Park land. Source: author.

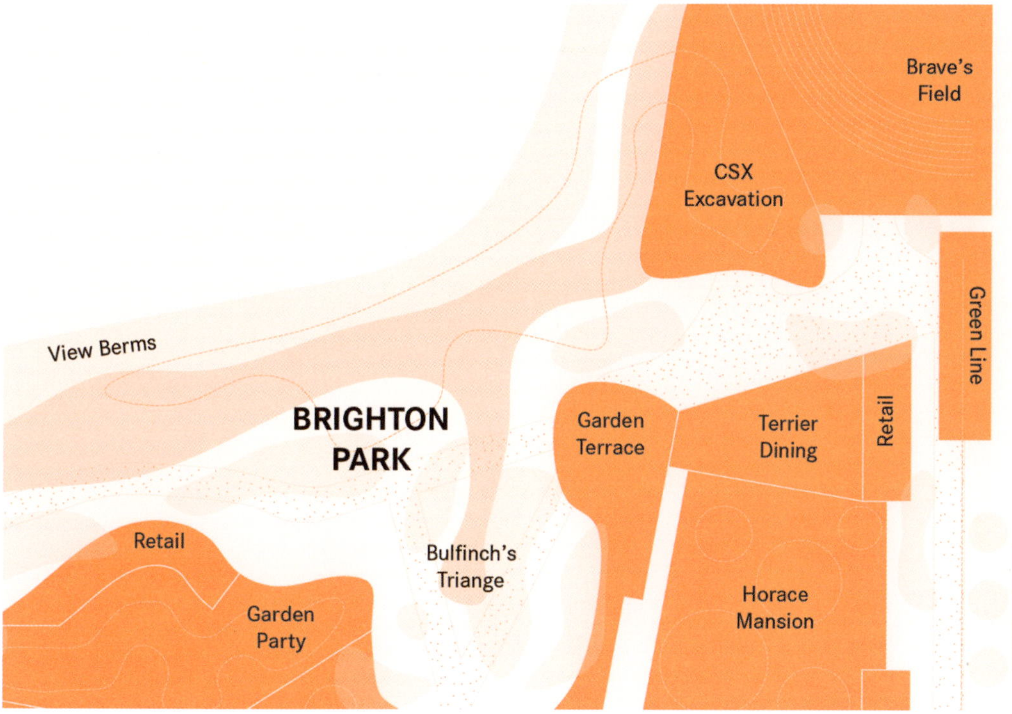

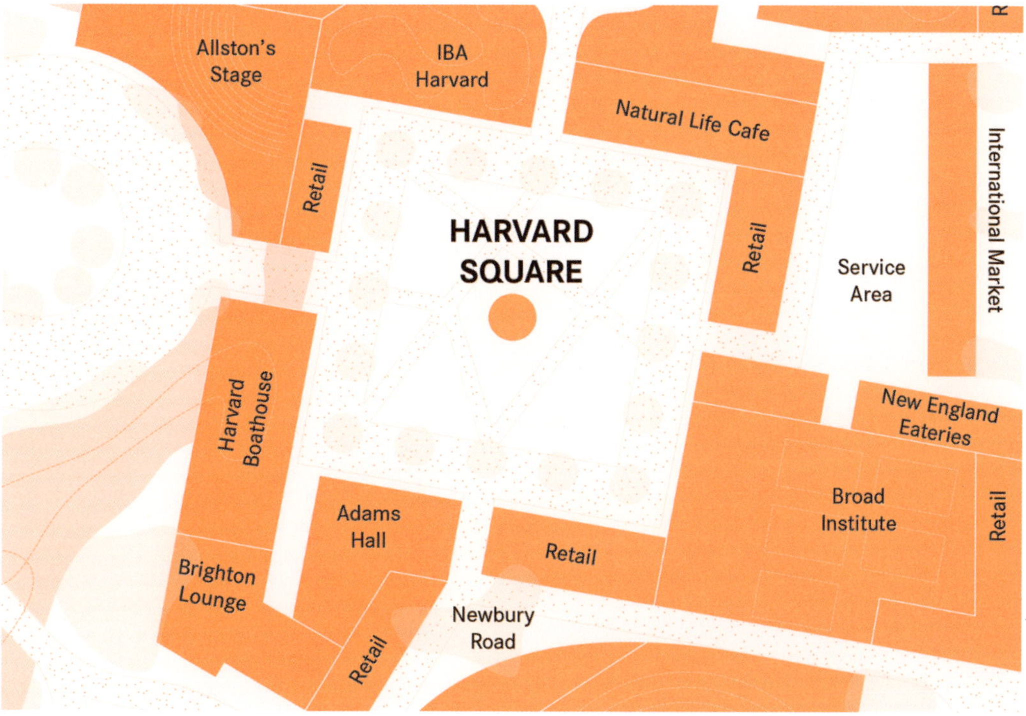

This page and next page: Details of plans for selected lands within Allstonland, including Brighton Park, Harvard Square, and Charles River Circle. Source: author.

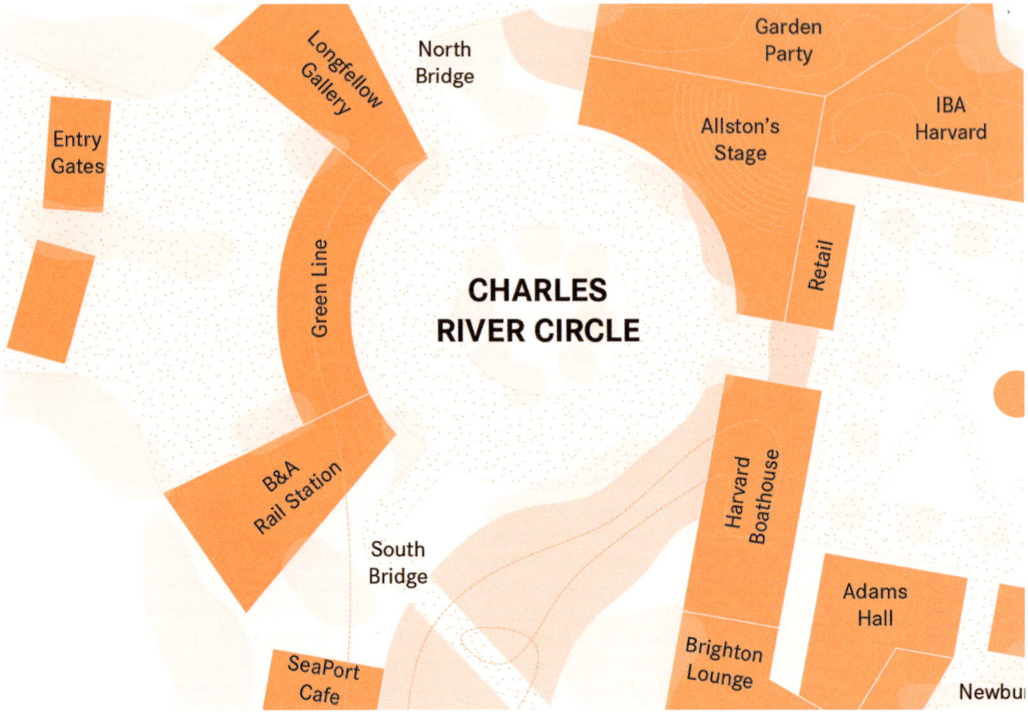

network, and other registers, but not so much as to become meaningless for design or our everyday experience.

Other considerations abound. With regard to urban design, all Disney parks tend to fall into either an axial organization (like most of the Magic Kingdom parks) or a clustered organization (like many of the parks that are paired with a Magic Kingdom park), as diagrammed in Chapter 3. Accordingly, Allstonland is clustered as Hong Kong Disneyland's foil and has experiences grouped into the key urban groupings in Allston: the Charles River, Harvard University, Comm Ave, Harvard Ave, Packard's Corner, and Brighton Park. Each of these lands has its experiences divided among restaurants, quick eats, shops, "flipper" rides, shows, and tent-pole rides and attractions. Furthermore, the architectural considerations are particular: façade treatments are critical, as are space requirements and the relationship of public fantasy to required hidden service areas—infrastructure.

Here, after isolating experience and structure, we also have the freedom to make form into its ideal shape. For example, in light of Harvard's transmogrification, why not correct the age-old error of Harvard Square's name—that there is, in fact, no square—and make a Harvard Square land which is a literal square? Or a circle an actual circle, a corner an actual corner? Such a powerfully Platonic form suggests the potential of the exercise, as well as heightens our productive absurd-plausible dichotomy.

In the end, these are some takeaways that we can extract from our displacement thought experiment: a clustered urban structure with spatial relations considered alongside use and program might serve Allston well; the landscape of Allston's cultural content can be isolated, understood, and experientially re-created in the public realm; and these experiences can be formed based on Platonic ideals. Here we aim at no less a target than to transform Allston into its ideal form.

Full plan for Allstonland, an approximate translation of Allston, displaced into Hong Kong as a theme park, including a diagram of Platonic forms extracted from its lands. Source: author.

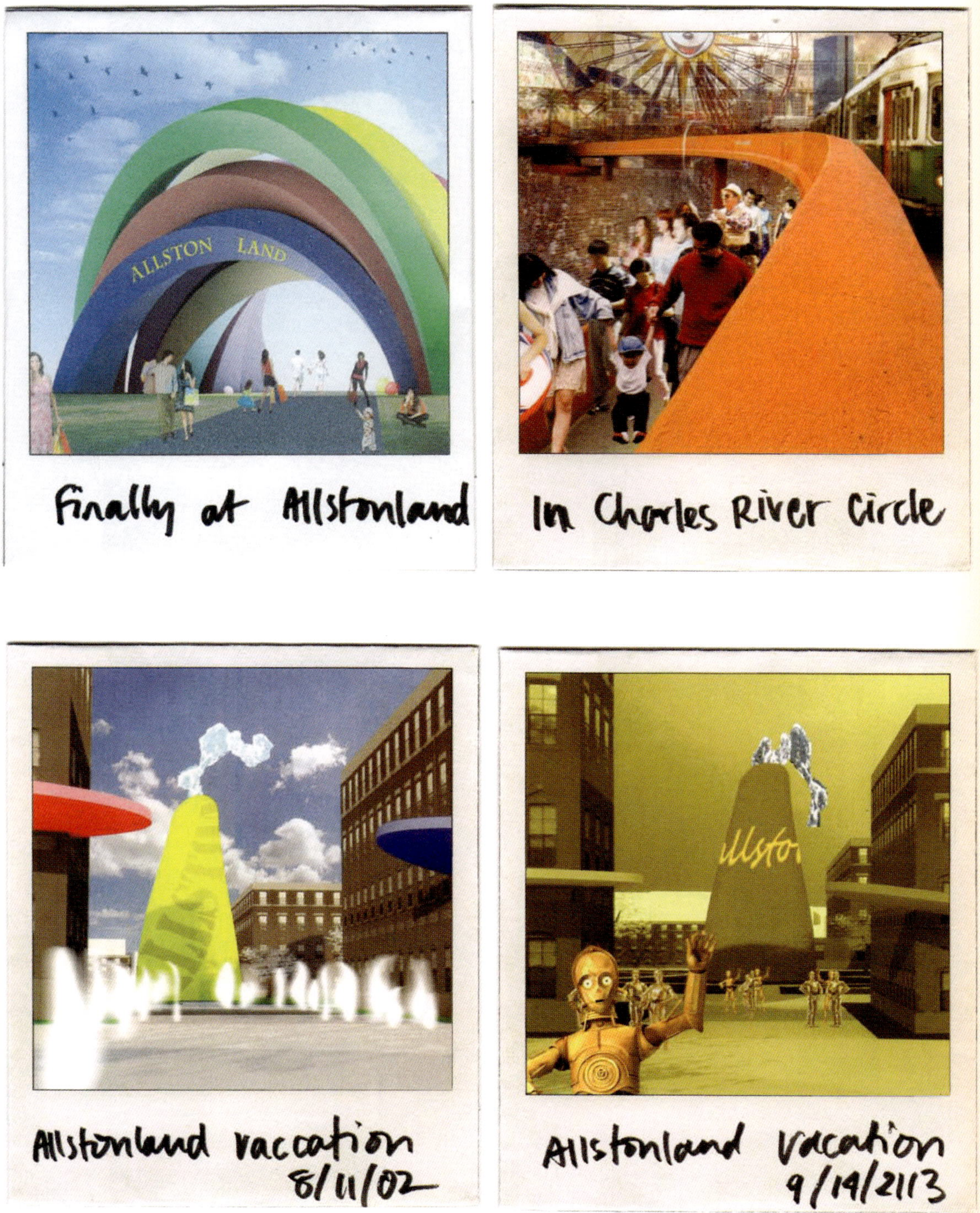

Polaroids of approximate translation in action. These renderings were produced by the author in collaboration with a number of other designers, and are placed as short interludes in between each chapter. These particular Polaroids were created in collaboration with Enas AlKhudairy, Nate Imai, and Ann Woods. Source: author.

These particular Polaroids were created in collaboration with Midori Mizuhara, Kyle Barker, Joshua Choi, and Karina Silvester. Source: author.

These particular Polaroids were created in collaboration with Kyle Barker, Rena Yang, Stephen Fan, and Slobodan Radoman. Source: author.

Chapter 5

Approaching Infinity: Strip Malls as Los Angeles's Manhattan Grid

Allow me, if you will, to take us on a small detour. Strip malls, believe it or not, can help us better understand how to arrive at Allston's ideal form and can also teach us a lot about urban design. Strip malls, while being a ubiquitous feature of contemporary cities around the globe, often evade thorough consideration in urban planning discussions. One of the few academic journal articles to critically analyze strip malls in any depth is a 2012 publication by Orly Linovsky where she notes the strip mall's attractive qualities, such as low rental costs to immigrant entrepreneurs and other small business owners, which have been unfortunately overlooked by a "design-centric" planning culture.[1] Other scholars, as well, have noted strip commercial development's importance to ethnic and immigrant commerce despite their maligned reputation and aesthetics.[2]

1 Orly Linovski, "Beyond Aesthetics: Assessing the Value of Strip Mall Retail in Toronto," *Journal of Urban Design* 17, no. 1 (2012): 81–99, https://doi.org/10.1080/13574809.2011.646247.

2 Anastasia Loukaitou-Sideris, "Regeneration of Urban Commercial Strips: Ethnicity and Space in Three Los Angeles Neighborhoods," *Journal of Architectural and Planning Research* 19, no.4 (2002): 334–350.

Beyond their importance to entrepreneurs based on accessibility and low rental costs, I argue that these spaces create a micro-community within them due to their small size and site design. Typically arranged in an "L" or "U" shape on a relatively small lot with street-facing parking, strip malls create a kind of outdoor room that allows its inhabitants to view, consider, and engage with one another. Lauren Berlant has described the emergence of an "intimate public" when analyzing "women's culture,"an affective phenomenon wherein masses of people with nearly nothing in common still co-identify with each other because of largely imagined similarities.[3] So too do strip mall inhabitants exhibit the qualities of an intimate public, cohering a shared identity over a compressed physical space and similar complaints around landlords or customers. Far from strip malls being a merely utilitarian urban space, they can actually generate public intimacies that bind cities together.

Another way that strip malls contribute to urban life is precisely because of their generic spatial and design qualities: they offer a rhizomatic expansion of small spaces that can expand into every spare contour of the city, offering a nearly infinite scaffolding for every imaginable activity. While most have decried the mundane, banal, generic stucco boxes that blight street corners with yet another laundromat and tailor, what gets overlooked is the way that this design approach enables rapid growth for new urban space that can be as easily adapted for use as churches, fitness centers, and experimental pop-ups as it is for the famed donut shops so common in Los Angeles strip malls. I see this "no style" quality as enabling a design ethos of "approaching infinity," which I will discuss later in this chapter.

A similar set of ideas can be seen in Rem Koolhaas's *Delirious New York*, where the author posits that Manhattan's meticulously ordered street grid enables boundless possibilities within it and a "deliriousness" of unexpected uses co-locating.[4] It is, in fact, the very generic, mundane quality of the street grid, the simplest of urban plans, that engenders the delightful chaos that we associate with urban life in New York City. Strip malls are, in a way, the ordered street grid of Los Angeles and the countless other cities in which they proliferate, generating a delirious quality when, say, a white cube art gallery locates next to a donut shop. Both grid and strip mall are formal structures that are able to act as a container for all sorts of urban narratives, events, uses, and other messy realities that make cities so exciting and urban design so challenging. The benefits of this kind of urbanism go beyond providing a container for a multitude of uses; they also create space and belonging for a multitude of people from all kinds of cultures and backgrounds.

In this chapter, we will delve deeper into the history of strip malls and consider how the concepts of "no style" and "approaching infinity" can inform urban design practice, with Manhattan's grid and Los Angeles's strip malls as case studies. The delirious quality that these prototypical urban forms can provide give yet another valuable urban design lesson for our intervention into Allston and its various approximate translations.

3 Lauren Berlant, *The Female Complaint: The Unfinished Business of Sentimentality in American Culture* (Durham: Duke University Press, 2008).

4 Rem Koolhaas, *Delirious New York: A Retroactive Manifesto for Manhattan* (New York: The Monacelli Press, 1997).

The Beginnings of the Strip Mall

What is a strip mall? If any entity has a grasp of the typology, it would most certainly be La Mancha Development Corporation, the single largest developer of strip malls in Southern California—it has built around 1,400 strip malls since 1973. In an interview I conducted in 2017 with Sam Bachner, the long-time president of La Mancha, he defined strip malls by "their convenience provided to a localized community through access to small shops and services and easy parking and pedestrian walking distances." For this reason, Bachner and other developers prefer the "convenience center" nomenclature, while news organizations and public agencies often default to the generic term "mini-mall." I use the term "strip mall" because it is the term most popularly used in vernacular language and is most easily understood, and it is also the term that best encapsulates the often pejorative connotations related to the building type, making it a term worth recuperating.

We can identify strip malls based on a specific set of architectural and morphological criteria. Bachner notes the importance of street-facing parking and pedestrian access, small size, and local market. The International Council of Shopping Centers, a trade group, defines "strip/convenience" shopping centers as having a trade area of less than a mile radius, as possessing no major anchors apart from possibly a convenience store, and as built on a site of under three acres with under 30,000 square feet of gross leasable area.[5] According to the Los Angeles Municipal Code, developed during the backlash to widespread construction of strip malls in the 1980s, they are defined as having a site less than 65,000 square feet, or about one and a half acres, with more than one retail establishment, and no more than three stories in height.[6]

5 See the ICSC "U.S. Shopping-Center Classification and Characteristics" published online at http://www.icsc.org.

6 See definition in LAMC § 12.03 for "Mini-Shopping Mall" and additional code requirements in LAMC § 12.22.A.23, accessible online at http://www.amlegal.com/codes/client/los-angeles_ca/.

Defining the Strip Mall

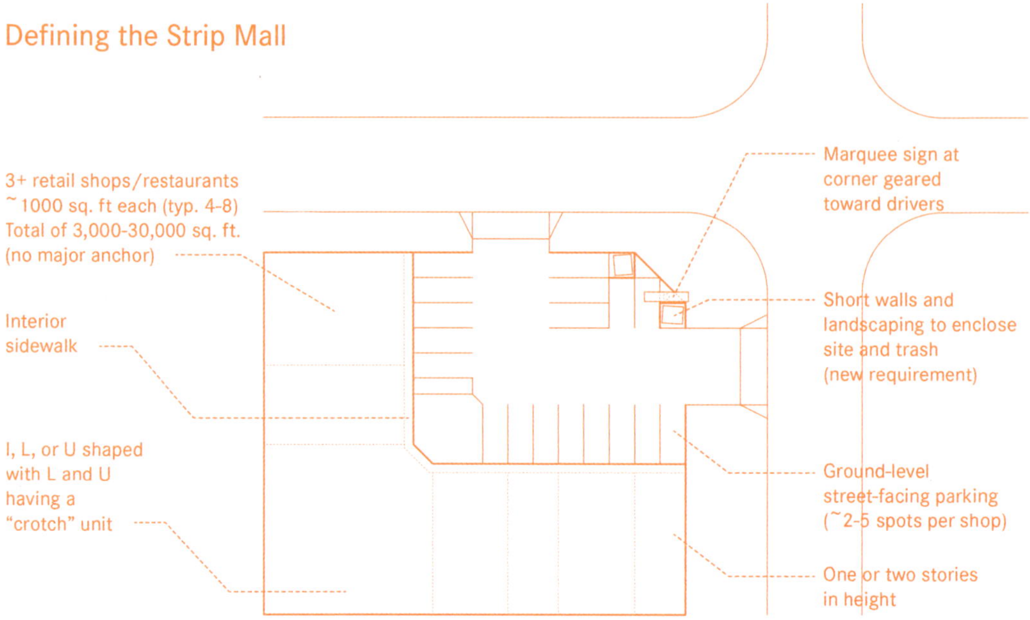

Diagram showing typical strip mall site plan. Source: author.

Based on the combination of these various definitions, I define a strip mall as a collection of at least three retail shops and restaurants of a small size, totaling 3,000 to 30,000 square feet, on a single site which has only ground level parking primarily facing the street. Using these criteria to map out the location of all the strip malls in the City of Los Angeles using GIS analysis and county assessor's data, I find that there are approximately 2,471 strip malls in total—a staggering number, even in the vast urban fabric of LA. This definition, however, goes beyond the quantitative architectural and morphological qualities that give rise to a particular building type and a realtor's sales pitch of convenience and low rental costs. Its spatial structure as driven by this relatively compact form, housing a dense and diverse array of shops, gives way to a unique sociality that is fundamental to the way strip malls have functioned as sites of ethnic and immigrant placemaking in urban life.

Based on several interviews and first-hand accounts, review of historical *Los Angeles Times* articles, review of public documents, and other scholarly and web sources, the history of strip malls in Los Angeles can be described as generally following three phases: their original design and development during the 1920s, their reinvention in the 1970s and subsequent backlash in the 1980s, and their current existence as sites with growing cultural cache and gentrification.

The strip mall was borne out of Los Angeles's historical techno-utopian car-oriented culture and has since been exported, usually with some degree of dismay, to nearly every city around the world in recently developed car-oriented urban fabric. While cities are left to grapple with the overall effects of car-oriented development, the strip mall has often been maligned as part of this urban transformation—a positioning that belies the cultural role it now plays in the ethnic communities of global cities, and the fact that many of them, at least in Los Angeles, have since turned into destinations for a largely pedestrian audience.

Strip malls were first built during the 1920s as "drive-in markets" with the advent of the automobile, and they were first developed and came to prominence in Los Angeles, which had a unique blend of easily available and developable land, as well as a large middle-class population of car-owning residents who had recently migrated from the Midwest. As Richard Longstreth has documented in his magisterial account of the design and development of car-oriented commercial space, the drive-in market was first conceived in 1923 by C. L. Peckham, the head of an insurance adjustment firm who was irked at the difficulty of finding parking at traditional Main Street-style commercial destinations.[7] His "Ye Market Place" was to be designed in a pleasing architectural style, with many shops so visitors could utilize the center as a "one-stop shop," located away from central locations but on a highly trafficked road, and in a "U" shape that allowed for maximum store frontage and a central courtyard for parking.

As Longstreth goes on to document, an L-shaped configuration at street corner lots of around 12,000 square feet with billboard signage and alleyway commercial loading became the dominant architectural configuration—strikingly consistent with the strip malls that were to be developed in future decades. Drive-in markets typically had multiple food-related vendors, and other uses included flower shops, pharmacies, gas stations, and laundry facilities. The architectural design and building aesthetics for drive-in markets in Los Angeles generally matched the neighborhood in which the market was situated: a Spanish style in Hollywood, art deco style along the modern Miracle Mile, or basic wood-framing in lower income areas. The building type saw a "meteoric ascent" during the 1920s and became the dominant commercial building type for developers until they saturated the landscape and the emergence of supermarket retail in the 1930s began to transform retail architecture yet again.[8]

7 For a complete account of the drive-in market as referenced here, see Richard Longstreth, "Stores the Road Passes Through," in *The Drive-in, the Supermarket, and the Transformation of Commercial Space in Los Angeles, 1914-1941* (Cambridge: MIT Press, 1999), 33–75.

8 Ibid., 37.

The Strip Mall Reborn

Strip malls returned to prominence during the oil crisis of the 1970s as scores of gas stations closed, once again starting in Los Angeles and then spreading to other locales around the world. These small corner parcels of land that once housed gas stations were commercially valuable due to their high visibility and access to vehicular traffic but remained relatively inexpensive as development sites. La Mancha, among a handful of other commercial real estate developers, snapped up these properties and transformed them into the modern strip mall: typically, an L-shaped building of around 5,000 square feet would sit at the back of the lot, housing around five retail shops or restaurants while a small, street-facing parking lot was located in the front.

The first of these were built by La Mancha in 1973 at 8969 Woodman Avenue in the San Fernando Valley. They quickly converted the gas station site, already zoned for commercial use, constructing a strip of retail spaces at the rear of the lot with a small parking lot at the front, with tenants including donut shops, massage parlors, and laundry facilities over the years. The design was minimal and generic, a rectangular box made from stick frame and block wall construction with room for illuminated signage. No style, to a tee. Its only adornment, to this day, is a faux mansard roof with red tile, perhaps a vague nod to Spanish-style architecture. Despite its lack of architectural innovation, 8969 Woodman Avenue, or at least by way of its key typological elements, was replicated thousands of times over in Southern California alone.

These humble commercial spaces were often considered ugly, but they became key sites for entrepreneurs who could afford them due to the low rental costs. In Los Angeles, these entrepreneurs were often immigrants who opened restaurants, beauty parlors and nail salons, donut shops, laundry facilities, and other such businesses—and strip mall development growth was coincident with rising post-1965 immigration rates. La Mancha made it a point to seek out immigrant entrepreneurs to fill leases: where larger developers saw a risk, the owners of La Mancha saw hardworking individuals that reminded them of their own parents' immigrant origins and the potential for a new real estate market within ethnic enclaves.[9] La Mancha also had a trick up its sleeve: a working development relationship with 7-Eleven which, during this period, had coincidentally decided to commence with a massive expansion and actively courted new immigrants as franchisees.[10] A 7-Eleven would often serve as an "anchor" tenant for these strip malls, with other mom and pop businesses filling out the remainder of the available space.

There was a backlash against their

9 See Judy Pasternak, "The Men of La Mancha," *Los Angeles Times*, September 28, 1986.

10 For more on these histories, see Mary Melton, "A Brief History of the Mini-Mall," *Los Angeles Times*, November 16, 1997; Bob Howard, "The Southern California Mini-Mall's Rise and Fall," *Los Angeles Times,* October 11, 1998; and Lauren Etter and Michael Smith, "The War Inside 7-Eleven," *Bloomberg Businessweek*, November 9, 2018.

The first modern strip mall, 8969 Woodman Avenue, built by La Mancha in Los Angeles's San Fernando Valley. Source: author.

proliferation in 1980s Los Angeles, which reached a fever pitch after about 1985, when they began to be referred to as "pod malls" in reference to *Revenge of the Body Snatchers*. Racial sentiment was often sublimated into discussions around strip malls as their rise tracked immigration patterns and their immigrant urbanism was often seen as unsightly and ugly. Reporters covering the backlash in the Eagle Rock neighborhood quoted residents who thought that strip malls would "threaten to destroy Eagle Rock's old-fashioned ambiance," and that they only wanted to "protect our community" by making sure that newcomers would "fit in."[11] In South Pasadena, residents saw strip malls "serving as a magnet for criminals and disrupting the tranquility of their neighborhoods."[12] And echoing his constituents' concerns regarding the retail developments, then-Councilmember Michael Woo for the Hollywood neighborhood stated that "they are unattractive and serve commuters rather than the people in the surrounding neighborhoods."[13]

While race and immigration status are not explicitly mentioned, language contrasting "old fashion ambiance" and "tranquil" community sensibilities with the "threat" of "criminal" activity and "unattractive" development for people from "other places" who wouldn't "fit in" is laden with racialized connotations. Scholar George Lipsitz has theorized the dominance of the "white spatial imaginary," which appears as an unquestioned normative baseline in the way our cities are conceptualized, capitalized, and distributed and this imaginary appears to be hard at work in how strip malls were maligned during this period. As Lipsitz describes, the white spatial imaginary need not be consciously performed for its impacts to flow to particular beneficiaries and not to others. And these impacts are material: the white spatial imaginary, "based on exclusivity and augmented exchange value, functions as a central mechanism for skewing opportunities and life chances in the United States along racial lines."[14] The desire to eliminate strip malls is a burden that would fall disproportionately upon the immigrant urbanisms borne out of them.

The three areas in Southern California which appear most often in the newspaper archives—Eagle Rock, South Pasadena, and Hollywood—took the first steps in setting up local moratoria on strip mall development in mid-1987, but even these were then superseded by a city-wide outright ban by late 1987 passed by the city council. The moratorium was originally intended to be temporary, but it ultimately dragged on for nearly two years as strip mall code requirements were debated, requiring then-mayor Tom Bradley to sign an extension ordinance into law.

New building code regulations were finally passed in 1989, which made their construction much more difficult. The new development requirements focused on providing greater quantities of parking, enclosures which would hide trash and other signs of life, significant amounts of landscaping and lighting, and signage which was much more discreet. These requirements pointed toward the sense that strip malls were dirty, dangerous, culturally "other," and needed to be self-contained so that their customers would not infringe upon surrounding uses. A combination of the new regulations, limited availability of land, and an economic downturn all but eliminated strip mall development. From the 1920s onward, around 250 strip malls were built in Los Angeles each decade, exploding to almost 600 during the '80s, and then rapidly tapering off to virtually zero as of today.

Only after strip mall development was all but eliminated were these unloved spaces reimagined as sites where unexpectedly good food could be found, and entrepreneurial creatives could afford cheap space—just as national conversations around diversity sparked a change in acceptable sentiments around race and ethnicity, not least of all catalyzed in Los Angeles after the 1992 LA Uprising. Beginning in the 2000s through today, through the influence of food culture, Yelp, and figures such as the late writer and critic Jonathan Gold, a wider audience of customers are now seeking out the delicious food and affordable services which are often offered in strip mall locations, giving them cultural cache. The *Los Angeles Times* goes from largely negative coverage of strip malls during the 1980s where burglaries, shady developers, derided architectural designs, and apocalyptic fires take center stage, to the 2000s where cultural figures write op-eds about the potential of these humble corner spaces, remodels are breathlessly covered, and a never-ending stream of surprised food critics note how good and cheap the cuisine is in strip malls.

This process will undoubtably play out in cities beyond Los Angeles as urban space worldwide has gone under the magnifying glass of social media influencers selling the latest "hidden gem" within an increasingly gentrified world. My ambivalence toward this mixed outcome—celebration of these important urban spaces just as they become difficult to build and increasingly expensive to rent—is instructive for urban designers as we consider the make-up of the ideal city. Is there an underlying logic to the strip mall that we can inject into our plans for the future of the city?[15]

11 Denise Hamilton, "Year Ban on Eagle Rock Mini-Malls Proposed," *Los Angeles Times*, February 26, 1987.

12 Edmund Newton, "South Pasadena Ban Aimed at Blocking Mini-Malls," *Los Angeles Times*, June 7, 1987.

13 Kenneth Fanucchi and Bob Pool, "Stall on Mini-Malls: Woo Seeks Moratorium on Downsized Shopping Malls," *Los Angeles Times*, April 2, 1987.

14 George Lipsitz, "The Racialization of Space and the Spatialization of Race: Theorizing the Hidden Architecture of Landscape," *Landscape Journal* 26, no. 1 (2007): 13.

15 For more recent research on the complexities and unique cultural value of the strip mall, which some of the content of this chapter was partially based, see Jonathan Jae-an Crisman, Alycia Cheng, and Annette Kim, "From Shopping Centers to Cultural Centers: Los Angeles Strip Malls as Sites of Ethnic and Immigrant Placemaking," *Urban Geography*, published ahead of print (2024): 1–31, https://doi.org/10.1080/02723638.2024.2337569.

In Praise of No Style

If we look at the landscape of strip malls juxtaposed against other high-rise buildings in Downtown Los Angeles, a particular quality of the strip mall becomes especially evident. There is one strip mall, or quasi-strip mall, in particular, where this juxtaposition stands out: Promenade Plaza retains the classic "L" shape of the strip mall with a heavily populated signboard but has a sunken plaza with seating where the parking lot ought to be, and a squat, linear apartment building sitting on top of the ground floor retail. Its generic, strip mall-like qualities stand in contrast to the iconicity of the building just across the street, Walt Disney Concert Hall, designed by Frank Gehry as a kind of belated antecedent to the Guggenheim Museum Bilbao which he designed in Spain. Promenade Plaza is actually one of a triptych, designed by architect Peter Kamnitzer along with the neighboring Promenade West and Promenade Towers developments, though Promenade Plaza is the only one to feature retail space, while the others are entirely residential. Kamnitzer believed in incorporating the natural landscape into urban spaces, perhaps even more than he believed in any sense of formal articulation for the buildings he designed, a stark contrast indeed to the undulations of Gehry's building across the street.

Nearly every architect that is practicing today—and, in fact, every designer in general—has a particular style much in the way that Gehry does. It is their fingerprint, their signature. It is the commodity that they offer to the world, be it a building, a spoon or other object, or an idea in their style. Zaha Hadid might be sort of swooshy and primarily continuous, while Thom Mayne has corners and vaguely fabrication-y styled building parts. Vivienne Westwood is giving punk to a UK lineage (with a healthy dose of tartan), where Virgil Abloh (also a trained architect) is giving streetwear meets high fashion with a touch of Duchamp. But what does this do when we bleed over into the social world? How does style translate into human connection, or into urban space? It is not an easy task.

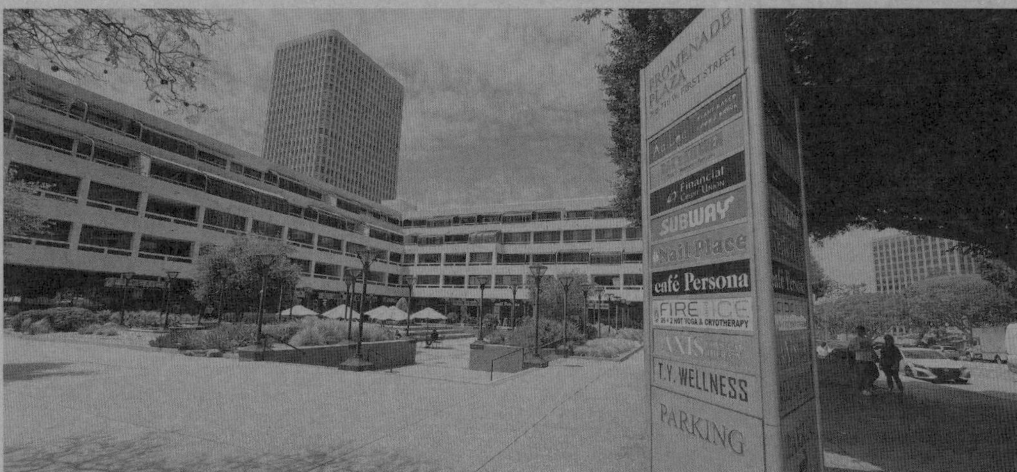

Peter Kamnitzer's Promenade Plaza and its strip mall-like ground floor retail. Source: author.

Frank Gehry's Walt Disney Concert Hall across the street from Promenade Plaza. Source: author.

Interestingly, even the most stylized of designers often find themselves at a loss when approached with the task of urban planning. There are a few potential options: design an inordinately large building with the signature style, scaling up beyond sensibility as Bjarke Ingels and his BIG firm might do. Or design an urban detail as a pattern, a motif that is replicated endlessly on everything from bus stops to paver tiles. Or, perhaps, attempt to inscribe one's style into a planometric design and hope that it remains evident for those on the ground rather than only those who fly overhead by helicopter or airplane. Each of these possibilities offers a slim chance of interesting success and a decent likelihood of disastrous failure.

An entirely alternative proposal might be the radical approach that has been unwittingly used since urban design received a name: to abandon style altogether. This certainly is not an approach that is used intentionally, and similarly many notable plans are quite intentional in forcing style upon the ground, be it through one of the aforementioned methods or another. Yet in some of the best, understated urban planning, one finds no style at all. Consider, for example, the New York City street grid, borne out of the Commissioners' Plan of 1811: a simple gridiron pattern of roads and plats, natural topography be damned.

How does one design without style, and how might one use such a practice with intention and across other scales and scopes? As it turns out, participatory processes tend toward no style due to their inherently conflicting inputs toward ideal outcomes. As the Polaroid images developed for the New Allston project inserted throughout this volume suggest, having no style turns out to make a strong comment indeed. Each coming from the hand of a different person with a different experience of the project, these micro-narratives make a composite whole that is far more complex and rich than what one designer could ever create on their own.

If we return to our example of Promenade Plaza, you can observe how style isn't exactly the point. Instead, we consider functional aspects like street frontage and seating in the exterior plaza, massing that privileges light and exterior space over aesthetics of style and form, and above all how all these things impact daily use for a building's users and inhabitants.

"No style" is something of a philosophical statement. It might mean a defense of minimalism. Less is more, emptiness holds the possibility of being filled, and good design is as little design as possible—so say Ludwig Mies van der Rohe, Kenya Hara, and Dieter Rams.[16] But then every once in a while, things need to be a little punchier, they need some panache, so maybe "no style" is the championing of a sans elegance, raw and a bit tacky. Glitch art right after Braun, or perhaps the mystifying delight one finds in the work of FAT, WAM, or Freddy Mamani. Indeed, different modes of action are appropriate for different situations. Then "no style" means just that: freeing oneself from being beholden to the confines of any particular style, allowing you to have the solution that is always just about right for the particular context and people that you are designing for.

Strip malls, too, have their own sensibility sans style. While Promenade Plaza is not a classic strip mall, per se, it is nevertheless instructive in how strip mall-esque architecture eschews style in favor of generic, functional, and urbane qualities. Form follows function doesn't quite capture the whole essence of this "no style" approach since form still plays a role. If we were to get biblical, we might consider the old adage "the meek shall inherit the earth": we have a design that isn't trying to get in your face but, rather, blend into its urban surroundings and serve its users and ultimately make life as decent as possible for as many people as possible. Blessed are the strip malls and, indeed, they have multiplied.

16 Philip Johnson, *Mies van der Rohe* (New York: Museum of Modern Art, 1947); Kenya Hara, *Designing Design* (Baden: Lars Muller, 2011); and Dieter Rams, *Less but Better* (Germany: Jo Klatt Design + Design Verlag, 1995).

Approaching Infinity

In the same way that having no style lends itself toward a broad acceptance of any potential design solution, so too does having a radical openness toward all other elements of design, and indeed even the people, places, and things that go into the designs or use them on a daily basis. Like the secret of the French language, that more or less all the verbs can (irritatingly) be conceived of as *irréguliers*, design demands the pragmatic acceptance of solutions that are unexpected, unorthodox, or perhaps even a bit ugly. The most beautiful design isn't very beautiful at all if it doesn't work. *Et comme le français*, a patchwork pragmatism turns out to be one of the most beautiful things of all.

While inconsistencies in certain elements of design can derail a solution, those same inconsistencies can become part of a larger pattern, intrinsic to the identity of a design. Like examining a portion of a mosaic at close range, or a highly zoomed-in photograph, chaos can turn into order upon a recalibration of scale and perspective. And if each of these tesserae holds individual worth, their totality often turns out to be far more valuable than the sum of their parts. One moves from shards of glass to the Hagia Sophia in short order. This approach is one of working toward infinity: when the big picture can unite any number of individually valuable yet wholly disparate pieces, their value becomes exponentially more powerful as it aggregates.

In a way, this works much in the same way as it does for society. Political philosopher Iris Marion Young, in her writings on the importance of a "politics of difference," noted that "the unoppressive city is thus defined as openness to unassimilated otherness." [17] Young was reflecting on how the homogenizing tendencies within the social notion of "community" and identitarian politics at large were problematic because of how they demanded assimilation and adherence to communally dictated norms. The city, instead, engenders a "kind of relationship" between people that allows for relating to those utterly different from oneself within a temporal and spatial context that Young describes as "an experience of aesthetic

17 Iris Marion Young, "The Ideal of Community and the Politics of Difference," *Social Theory and Practice* 12, no. 1 (1986): 22.

inexhaustibility." This queer sensibility is part and parcel of the idea of approaching infinity: by rejecting adherence to a style, by being radically open to any potential design, you enable the creation of a diversity of spaces that allow for difference and infinite possibility.

In our contemporary society where meta-narratives have largely been discredited as myths that hold little truth for daily life—and for good reason—approaching infinity offers a means toward a narrative that transcends our Balkanized culture. Rather than the dogma of meta-narrative, you have a kind of narrative form that is defined by "aesthetic inexhaustibility." Applied to urban design practice, it becomes, in a sense, a politics of difference. In the rarefied arena of architectural theory, much ado has been made about the present dearth of polemics, positions, and projects. Something called "post-criticality" has crept in, replacing beliefs and manifestos with a sort of fuzzy acceptance of anything that can be properly framed within the pseudo-scientific terms of logic, order, and iteration.[18] The most problematic proposal is fine so long as it follows its own rules. Often, such proposals engage the social by hoping to reorganize society rather than serve society's needs. There is something in this complaint that theorists have called post-criticality that is, under the hood, a relatively conservative imaginary that longs for a past era of grand truths shared by all, a hope that perhaps these smaller projects can grow and evolve into a meta-narrative of old.

Even now, however, I cannot in good faith suggest that one or another of these projects are not without any merit, even if only on their own terms—and even if those terms exist nowhere outside their limited reality. But in contrast to the long-held belief that "projective practice," let alone staking out a position, is a zero-sum game that necessarily excludes other alternatives, approaching infinity provides a third path. If one assumes that each project, each proposal, and each position contains at the very least a shred of truth, one comes at a total truth not through finding the "truthiest" of the projects but, rather, radically accepting and incorporating everything in a snowballing, momentous behemoth. This is a far cry from relativism, or even an "I'm okay, you're okay." It is, in fact, a radical position and perhaps the only truly radical position left. It isn't all or nothing; it is *all and everything—and forcefully so!*

All of this, as you might be surprised to learn, brings us back to the strip mall. It is an architectural or urban design strategy for approaching infinity. Within its humble design is the seed for infinite and inexhaustible reproducibility, but not a monoculture like a Cavendish banana waiting for disease to spell its extinction. Rather, each new strip mall, a simple copy-paste of that street-facing layout and its small, stucco boxes, enables infinite possibility within and around it, enabling signage, usage, and minor design variation that, somehow, allow just about anything you can imagine to inhabit it.

18 I am being overly flippant here, and perhaps it's a bit of a dead horse at this point, but old debates die hard. See Robert Somol and Sarah Whiting, "Notes around the Doppler Effect and Other Moods of Modernism," *Perspecta* 33 (2002): 72–77; Lara Schrijver, "Whatever Happened to Projective Architecture? Rethinking the Expertise of the Architect," *Footprint* 4 (2009): 123–127.

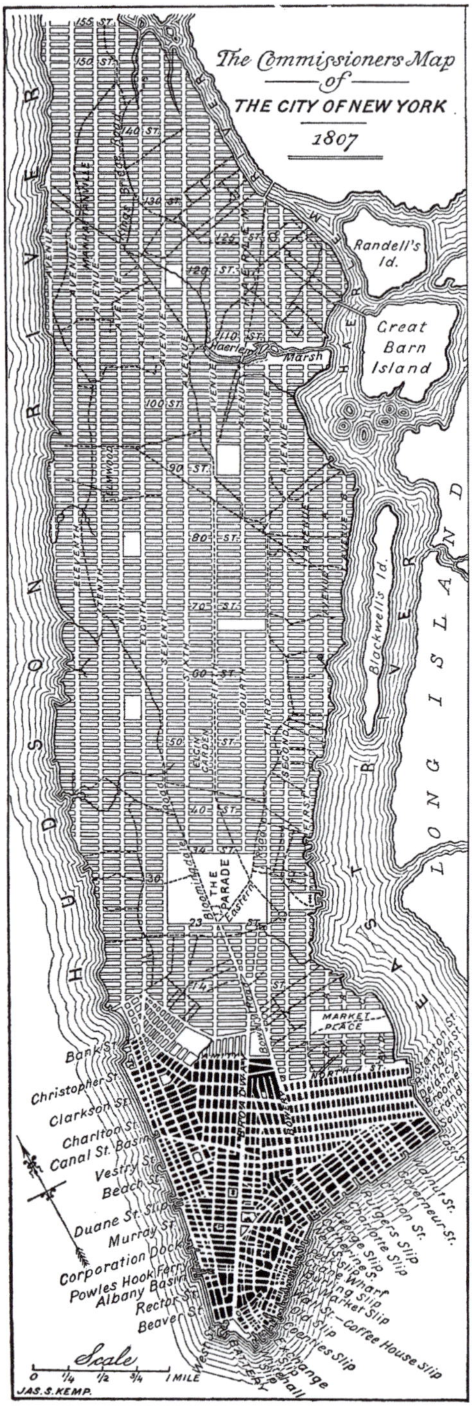

The Commissioners Plan of 1811, as drawn up a few years before it was adopted. Source: Harper's New Monthly Magazine, June 1893.

Koolhaas described this quality of the New York grid as a kind of "deliriousness," a generic and reproducible space within urban contexts that allowed for almost unimaginable difference, delight, and variation across its thousands of mostly identical, long-ish city blocks of about 200 feet wide—that is, in the up and downtown direction—and varying lengths of between 610-920 feet in the crosstown direction. Koolhaas, in his typical polemic writing, proclaimed that "All blocks are the same; their equivalence invalidates, at once, all the systems of articulation and differentiation that have guided the design of traditional cities." [19] In some sense, the more generic the city is, the more it allows for diversity of its inhabitants and their actions. Conversely, the more an urban plan or the architecture of a space forces itself upon you, the less you're able to move, be, or connect with others within that space.

Strip malls, in their mundane, generic, open-armed spatial quality, allow people with utterly different cultures, politics, businesses, and ways of being enter into a kind of intimacy with one another, connecting over the shared lore of local politics or perhaps uniting against a pesky landlord and, in turn, imagining worlds of shared identity that can bind these neighbors together. It is very much in line with what Lauren Berlant describes as "intimate publics," a world of shared identity and intimacy, however imagined, because of certain shared markers that can be registered in space.[20] Strip malls are a vehicle for delirious possibility, for approaching infinity, and for an emotional attachment that enables a politics of difference—all heady goals when designing the city of tomorrow.

19 Koolhaas, *Delirious New York*, 20.

20 Berlant, *The Female Complaint*, 5.

Polaroids of approximate translation in action. These particular Polaroids were created in collaboration with Richard Ong, Jared Press, Stephanie Warren, and Alice Shay. Source: author.

These particular Polaroids were created in collaboration with Irina Chernakova, Kyle Barker, Alexis Wheeler, and Eric Morris. Source: author.

The CSX Excavation

Harvard Square – Starting at HBS!

Brighton Development – our new home '14

H. Sq. Façade...

These particular Polaroids were created in collaboration with Colleen McHugh, SunMin Hwang, Tyler Crain, and Jasper Campsure. Source: author.

The ideal forms of New Allston: reconstructing Allstonland back into Allston using theories of forms, ideal forms, and megaforms discussed in the next chapter. Source: author.

Reconstruction: Chapter 6

The Ideal Forms of New Allston

What is the essence of a strip mall? Another way of asking that question is, what is the ideal form of a strip mall? Plato's theory of Forms is a metaphysics philosophy based on the idea that ideally formed mental abstractions are the truest essence of a thing, while the particular objects we see in reality are only copies of those abstractions.[1] For example, our idea of a square is four perfectly drawn lines of the exact same length with perpendicular identical angles that add up to 360 degrees. In reality, however, every attempt to draw this perfect square will fall short of the ideal, no matter how close. Proclus, a student of Plato's, suggested that these Forms are the essence of beauty, and later readers of Proclus imagined them as thoughts in the mind of God.[2]

Such thinking is related to the development of the five Platonic solids whose symmetry and perfection have made them into paradigms of aesthetic beauty. Each a polyhedron, which has the same number of faces meeting at each vertex, the Platonic solids were suggested to be the building blocks of the classical elements of air, earth, fire, water, and aether. Indeed, there are only five Platonic solids: the tetrahedron, the hexahedron, the octahedron, the dodecahedron, and the icosahedron.

The goal of any formal project whose aim is social uplift is, in fact, the identification and implementation of forms ideal for the situation in question. This can take many appearances depending on the media in use. Antiquity had its orders coming from on high, Le Corbusier's purism aimed at its own kind of purity, ergonomics reigns in one school of product design, and the mathematics of finance have their model state of balance and growth.

So, the ideal form of the strip mall would be its uttermost essence, boiled down to a state of pure abstract perfection such that no actual strip mall exactly fit the mold—and, at the same time, every strip mall is in some way a sort of copy of this ideal form. We know that strip malls most often take an "L," "I," or "U" shape in plan,

1 "Forms" is typically capitalized to make specific reference to the philosophical construct.

2 Pieter d'Hoine and Marije Martijn, eds., *All From One: A Guide to Proclus* (Oxford: Oxford University Press, 2017).

and include a small street-facing parking lot at their front. But I would argue that there are certain qualities of the strip mall that are also fundamental to their essence, namely, that they include a variety of small commercial spaces that allow for infinite possibility within them, they generate a kind of delirious quality even as they also produce a neighborly sense of public intimacy through their courtyard-like form in plan.

Designers are often presented with a paralyzing reality: the need to start designing something in the absence of what feels like solid ground to push off from. While there are countless ways to overcome this conundrum, one possible approach that can be especially productive for urban designers is to begin with an ideal form. It feels almost silly or childlike to take a complex urban site and then to draw something like a circle—or, perhaps, an "L," "I," or "U" shape. But, as we know from the humble strip mall, a little can go a very long way.

Beyond all we can learn from the strip mall about how to better design urban space, I suggest that we begin our next phase of approximate translation by considering what ideal forms might offer our displaced and thematized urban design for Allston, seeing what we can learn along the way.

The five Platonic solids, illustrated with their associated elements, drawn by Johannes Kepler in his 1619 book Harmonices Mundi. *Source: Smithsonian collection at archive.org, ioanniskepplerih00kepl.*

Replacement and Reconstruction

We last left Allston "displaced" into a version of itself as a Hong Kong theme park. The notion of displacement and defamiliarization has something in common with another set of literary and architectural ideas, deconstruction and deconstructivism. Deconstruction, most famously espoused by philosopher Jacques Derrida, was precisely an attempt to turn away from ideal forms, though within the realm of language and meaning. Instead of having some true, fixed essence, words only gain meaning and, in turn, their essence through their relationship and proximity to other words around them.[3]

Translation surfaces here too; in the same way that the spatial turn had literary scholars think seriously about space, so too has the textual turn in architecture, including this emphasis on deconstruction, allowed designers to incorporate new critical perspectives into their projects, constructing not only buildings but also intentionally constructing meaning within the urban landscape.[4] Deconstructing anything—from a work of literature to a building or an entire city—is illuminating because it reveals hidden meanings and underlying patterns. We can learn more about the nuances and motivations underlying the development of buildings, literature, and cities if we take them apart and analyze them.

Indeed, architects took up this project in the 1980s to incorporate Derrida's ideas into design. While Robert Venturi and Denise Scott Brown had been thinking about the role of semiotics in architecture for some time prior, the connection was made more concrete with Peter Eisenman's actual collaboration with Derrida for their 1982 submission to the Parc de la Villette design competition in Paris.[5]

Their "Chora L Works" proposal did two things: first, it referenced contextual elements in space including then-current site conditions as well as the abattoir that occupied the site in 1867 and the Paris city walls of 1848 and, second, it abstracted typically ordered elements of park design down into almost linguistic elements that were then formally manipulated in reference to those past and present site conditions. In other words, Eisenman and Derrida took architectural form as a kind of language that could be manipulated to generate contextual meaning.

This approach enabled the generation of novel and compelling formal possibilities but, at the same time, it abandoned the ordered rules of classical and modernist architecture. Not coincidentally, it came to be referred to as "deconstructivist" or "decon" architecture as a nod to not only deconstruction but also to the Russian Constructivist school of design from the

3 Jacques Derrida, *Of Grammatology* (Baltimore: Johns Hopkins University Press, 1976).

4 Tereza Topolovská. "Reading Buildings: The Textual Turn of Architecture as a Parallel to the Spatial Turn in Literary Studies," *Ars Aeterna 14*, no. 1 (2022): 58–70, https://doi.org/10.2478/aa-2022-0006.

5 Robert Venturi, Denise Scott Brown, and Steven Izenour, *Learning from Las Vegas* (Cambridge: MIT Press, 1972); Jacques Derrida and Peter Eisenman, *Chora L Works* (New York: Monacelli Press, 1997).

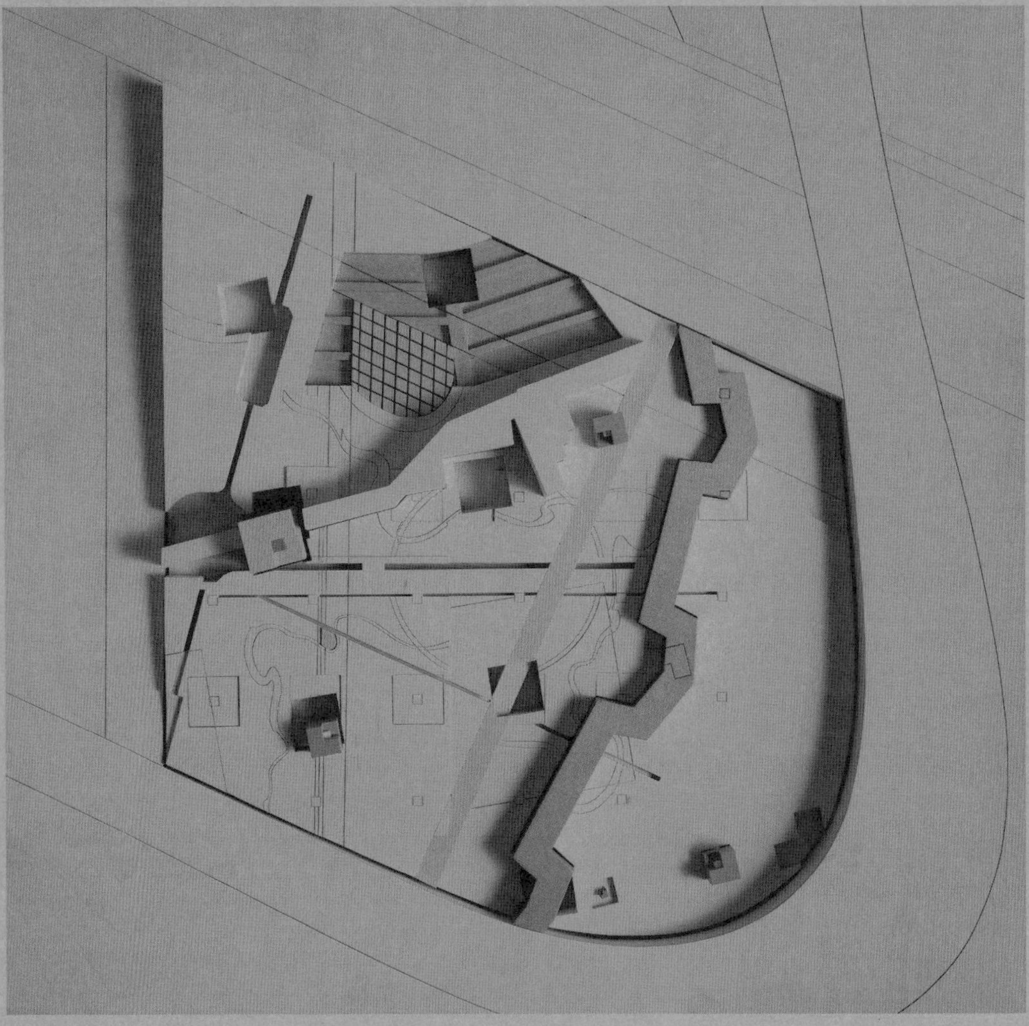

Model of Peter Eisenman and Jacques Derrida's Chora L Works proposal for the Parc de la Villette in Paris, 1982. Source: Peter Eisenman fonds, Canadian Centre for Architecture.

1920s which explicitly sought to highlight and celebrate the construction technologies of the industrial world. In this sense, deconstructivist architecture sought to move away from or even break apart the "essence" or "order" of architecture which had always been fundamentally based on the necessities of construction—columns, arches, and the like—and in so doing, move architecture into a conceptual realm of semiotic meaning.

Ironically, the underlying impetus of the project of deconstructivism is to evacuate architectural (i.e., construction-centric) meaning, while deconstruction was a philosophical project of creating a more grounded linguistic meaning. The two are so intertwined yet are hardly the same, almost opposites. And, moreover, the bigger possibility borne out of deconstruction is the very notion that so much of our world is, indeed, constructed—a fact that is often lost on deconstructivist architecture until it comes time to actually build. While its design ideas can be powerful as conceptual and process-oriented tools, it can often fall short when it comes time to "reconstruct" that which has been deconstructed. Worse still, later deconstructivst projects often relied on a kind of deconstructed stylistic approach, eschewing even the conceptual potential held by the movement—a reminder again that a "no style" approach is often a better approach. All of this is even more crucial when we consider the design of cities rather than of only a particular building or site.

This practice is well-illuminated in the thorny issues of historic preservation. Over the past decades, conservation moved beyond buildings to consider surrounding environments and contexts, ultimately landing on preservation of "historical urban landscapes" as the object of focus, despite this term's broad and vague nature. With the Vienna Memorandum and the Paris Recommendation that came out of UNESCO in 2005 and 2011, respectively, which established this concept, the necessity of some degree of change within preserved and historical environments was also acknowledged, as well the layering of the "cultural and natural values and attributes" that constitute these historical urban landscapes.[6] But these decisions leave many questions open: what are the limits of change, and how does one balance conservation with sustainable development? What, again, is the essential meaning of a place, and to what extent can it be changed while remaining true to itself?

If we return to Allson, then, and imagine that our act of displacement had some connection with deconstruction—we're unpacking the constructed meaning within the space, understanding its contextual relationships and constituent parts, and then putting it in a wholly new place where all of these meanings and relationships are pressure tested—then we can imagine "replacement" as a kind of act of reconstruction.

Displacement and deconstruction challenged Allston's traditional urban layouts by fragmenting them into separate and thematic "lands." Theme parks have mastered this technique, dividing their spaces into distinct realms to offer visitors diverse experiences. Allstonland, however, requires an act of replacement and reconstruction wherein we understand these distinct lands anew, where we can better understand their relationships and their essence, the limits of what we can change, and the requirements for what must

6 Arturo Azpeitia Santander, Agustín Azkarate Garai-Olaun, and Ander De la Fuente Arana, "Historic Urban Landscapes: A Review on Trends and Methodologies in the Urban Context of the 21st Century," *Sustainability* 10, no. 8 (2018): 2603, https://doi.org/10.3390/su10082603.

remain true to its original, putting these essential elements back into their spatial origins.

Displacement has another specific meaning within urban planning contexts. Whether from the forced relocation of urban renewal, the slow creep of gentrification, or other processes of urban change, people experience displacement tangibly when they are forced from their homes or communities. So deconstruction, too, comes with peril, even as it operates on the less tangible scale of signs and meaning. Cultural gentrification, in this sense, can be as powerful and disrupting as physical displacement.[7]

Cultural memory has been demonstrated as critical for urban denizens' sense of place, contributing as well to the kinds of historic urban landscapes that require protection. In one analysis of the demolished Masrah Al Salam theater in Alexandria, Egypt, researchers noted how the demolition was protested so heavily by local residents because of the deep ties that specific place had with their memories of growing up in the area.[8] As the building was destroyed, so too were their very memories placed at risk, spotlighting the fragility and ties to place of one's sense of self, identity, and life history.

Mass urban migration thus affects the intangible aspects of city life, such as community identity and shared memories. Displaced residents risk losing their cultural heritage and sense of belonging, highlighting the necessity for an integrated approach to urban development. Although deconstruction is useful for gaining insight into complicated systems, it demands reconstruction even when operating on a purely theoretical, hypothetical, or conceptual level. Thus, the term "reconstruction" includes more than merely the replacement of buildings or streets. It also requires repairing the social and cultural fabric of the area and making sure nothing important to that place, tangible or intangible, is lost.

Returning, then, to our project in Allston, the process of replacement and reconstruction involves taking the insights that we learned through the process of displacement and reintegrating them back into an actual urban design in our point of origin. We have distilled cultural and formal elements from Allston, from its urban histories of rock and roll and its critical programs and uses, to the underlying ideal forms that ought to make up its physical layout, such as the square or the yard. These are the essential elements to keep as we create a new urban plan for the neighborhood, the pieces that ensure a new design retains a connection to place, history, and culture for its residents and users. But, before we jump to representing these elements, the designers among us could likely use a bit more formal refinement, a more solid ground upon which to work. For this, let us dig a little deeper into what, exactly, the formal qualities of the urban design ought to consist of.

7 For more on this, see Jonathan Jae-an Crisman, "Art and the Aesthetics of Cultural Gentrification: The Cases of Boyle Heights and Little Tokyo in Los Angeles," in *Aesthetics of Gentrification: Seductive Spaces and Exclusive Communities in the Neoliberal City*, ed. Christoph Lindner and Gerardo Sandoval (Amsterdam: Amsterdam University Press, 2021), 137–154, https://doi.org/10.1515/9789048551170-008.

8 Fatmaelzahraa Hussein, John Stephens, and Reena Tiwari, "Cultural Memories and Sense of Place in Historic Urban Landscapes: The Case of Masrah Al Salam, the Demolished Theatre Context in Alexandria, Egypt," *Land* 9, no. 8 (2020): 264, https://doi.org/10.3390/land9080264.

Forms and Megaforms

The implications of the strip mall are thus: that if we are to approach a design with no style such that our users can approach infinity within them, we ought to design—at least from a formal sense—as little as possible. This is far easier for something at the scale of the strip mall, and a bit more difficult at the larger scales at which urban design operates. When confronted with the need to design something at this scale, it is tempting to treat the design process in a way similar to how one might approach a building: using the kinds of design language of structure, walls, openings, and ornament that typically result in a product of at least decent quality. But making design decisions at the urban scale demands a different kind of language, and certainly a lighter touch, as to ensure one's urban plan doesn't foreclose the possibility of everyday life within it. Theories of megaforms are instructive here for how to move forward and make formal decisions in the process of reconstruction.

Kenneth Frampton, in his 1999 Raoul Wallenberg Memorial Lecture, "Megaform as Urban Landscape," highlighted some of the historical antecedents and potentials of the megaform as a kind of organizing logic for design at very large scales.[9] First, as the global population grows and becomes increasingly urban, it becomes increasingly difficult to intervene in urban space in traditional (i.e., architectural) means of focus on urban cores or through code-based means like zoning. Instead, vast urbanized regions have emerged, typically with a great deal of less than ideal suburban and auto-centric development. Camillo Sitte, for example, as far back as 1889, noted the problem of "space-endlessness" and called for creating bounded forms at the urban scale.[10]

9 Kenneth Frampton, "Megaform as Urban Landscape," the Raoul Wallenberg Memorial Lecture given at The University of Michigan A. Alfred Taubman College of Architecture + Urban Planning on February 12, 1999, republished in *Journal of Delta Urbanism* 2 (2021): 14–23.

10 Camillo Sitte, *City Planning According to Artistic Principles* (New York: Random House, 1965 [1889]).

Kenzo Tange's 1960 Plan for Tokyo, showing a multi-use megaform that moves seamlessly from land to bay. Detail of photograph by Akio Kawasumi, 1961.

Second, as we have taken to the air, our perspective of urban spaces and landscapes transformed from a view on the ground to a topographical view in plan, opening up our awareness to different kinds of topologies and connections between urban forms and spaces. Frampton, here, gives the example of Le Corbusier's 1931 Plan Obus for Algiers that was imagined in relationship to the volcanic topographies that Le Corbusier purportedly observed from an aerial survey. Thus, Frampton provides a definition of megaforms based on five elements: a large, horizontal form (as opposed to vertical); complexity that is not defined by structural elements; a relationship to the existing urban landscape; integration into the existing natural topology; and a move toward densification.[11]

Frampton provides several possible examples: Henri Ciriani's concept of "un piece urbaine," Rafael Moneo and Manuel de Sola Morales's L'ilia Block in Barcelona, Vittorio Gregotti's concept of "the anthrogeographic landscape," Bruno Taut's concept of "the city crown," work from Hans Scharoun, Erich Mendelsohn, and others. But of particular note is Fumihiko Maki and Masato Ohtaka's concept of "collective form" in their analysis of Kenzo Tange's Tokyo Bay Project of 1960. Here, the permanence of megaform is accomplished through its ability to rapidly change, to accommodate different kinds of human needs as they evolve. And, later, Tange's work is noted for its attention toward topography, toward the undulating surface of the earth, and how relationship of above and below can provide grounds for programmatic and other sorts of design distinctions and possibilities.

Reyner Banham described Tange's plan as a "megastructure," though Frampton notes that the structure is less important than the particular qualities of the form: a megaform may include structural elements in its construction, but these are not as critical as the ways in which a megaform integrates with its surrounding urban and topological context.[12] For Tange, these elements included a linear core that stretched from one side of Tokyo Bay to the other, incorporating, in particular, civic and mobility uses. These not only connected to the surrounding geography, but the national economy, politics, and identity as well, coinciding with the Japanese government's plan for a national highway system.[13]

For our purposes, the megaform and, in particular, the ideal form of the megaform, can offer a kind of *no style* design system for creating space that is just what is needed and nothing more, creating open-ended space that can change as needs change, enabling inhabitants to create delirious, endless possibilities within its porous boundaries. Rather than a language of architecture, too often used within urban design, of structural elements, enclosure, and the like, instead we have a language based on responsive, topological form that enables the creation of urban space. Equally important are the ways in which these formal elements connect to broader considerations around sociopolitical and economic contexts.

11 Frampton, "Megaform as Urban Landscape," 18.

12 Reyner Banham, *Megastructure: Urban Futures of the Recent Past* (London: Thames and Hudson, 1976). Also useful for understanding Tange's Plan for Tokyo is Rem Koolhaas and Hans Ulrich Obrist, *Project Japan: Metabolism Talks* (Koln: Taschen, 2012).

13 Zhongjie Lin, "Urban Structure for the Expanding Metropolis: Kenzo Tange's 1960 Plan for Tokyo," *Journal of Architectural and Planning Research* 24, no. 2 (2007): 109–124; Hyunjung Cho, "Kenzō Tange's *A Plan for Tokyo*, 1960: A Plan for Urban Mobility," *arq* 22, no. 2 (2018): 139–150, https://doi.org/10.1017/S1359135518000301.

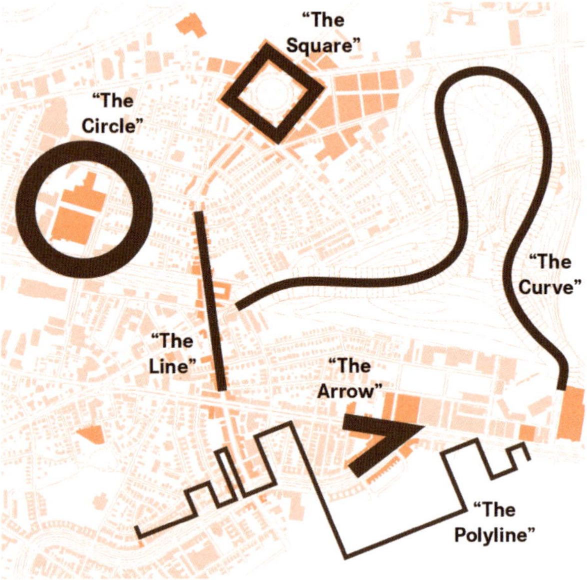

The ideal forms of New Allston, diagrammed.
Source: author.

Ideal Megaforms of New Allston

As we reconstruct Allston, we enact an approximate translation yet again. We went from a new urban design for Allston and displaced this design into a theme park design for Allstonland in Hong Kong. And now we go from Allstonland to New Allston, reconstructing the six “lands,” these core elements of the theme park, into a set of six ideal forms within Allston’s landscape. Taken together, they can be understood as a kind of megaform, though one, The Curve, is rightly a megaform in its own right.

New Allston can be understood as a first iteration, a kind of open-ended system that is meant to evolve and change over time. It is a “move fast and break things” design launch which can go through infinite approximate translations in the future. Its six ideal forms are themselves actually a matrix of ideal forms. Each comprises a formal design strategy matched with a programmatic strategy, two ideal forms interlocked with each other to create a platform for urban space and activity, much in the same way that the theme park lands operated, as spatial structure interlocked with mediatized programmatic system. The formal design strategies can all be utilized by urban designers, from massing based on a set of ideal forms, to a range of other slightly more “invasive” techniques including “Haussmannization” and historical district creation. Further, these ideal forms are the basis for their further surrealization, a process I discuss in Chapter 8 as a new kind of strategy for urban design representation that both incorporates and creates urban narratives in space. The ideal forms are as follows:

The Square, programmed as The Classroom, is actualized in a newly proposed Harvard Square development. A multi-level, mixed-use institutional development for Harvard's expansion includes retail, living, offices, a hotel, dorms, entertainment, classrooms, labs, and infinitely reprogrammable spaces. Six buildings, each of which has its interior arcade, rooftop exterior space, street frontage, and rear service and loading, comprise this megastructure. In this approach, densification means that Harvard's expansion need not continue outward, but can instead go vertical.

The Circle, programmed as The House, is actualized in the Media Circle Complex. The circle is made manifest by the radio waves that are emitted by this urban media infrastructure, like the rings that emanate out from a water drop. An interconnected topology of information sharing is created between WBZ, the Horace Mann School, and a new complex where the Boston Skating Club is relocating. Here there will also be open soundstages, studios, and event spaces, along with a production facility that loops in a ubiquitous sensing mesh that can capture live footage from anywhere in Allston, transforming inhabitants into active producers and performers, staging and scripting their mediatized reality with spaces that can be reutilized to meet the continuously changing media landscape.

The Curve, programmed as The Park, is actualized in a new type of infrastructure, Brighton Park. It is an elevated urban armature that touches down at either end, linking Lower Allston with the main portion of Allston across the Mass Pike. A central park, developable lots, an open-air chasm down to Mass Pike, a special-access road, and ancillary parks for residents comprise this unique, urban megaform. It operates like the second level of a building, almost doubling usable square footage, making urban space more affordable.

The Line, programmed as The Market, is actualized in the International Market Arcade. All of the existing buildings along Harvard Ave in the International Market Arcade will be "Haussmannized" with their façades trimmed and unified, a process of so-called "creative destruction." An open system of managed time-shares will allow the low-rent area to capitalize on its unique market and expand its internationally focused goods and sales, as well as act as a means for lower-income residents and recent migrants to find work and upward social and economic mobility in spaces that can be used for just about any commercial use imaginable. The strip mall, in a sense, becomes The Line.

The Polyline, programmed as The Stage, is actualized in the Rock City Corridor. A sound corridor made up of coordinated, hidden, directed audio emitters that weaves past all of the key Rock City venues in Allston creates a comprehensible urban fabric about this element of Allston's history—not least of all through this an invisible yet immensely present sonic scaffolding. This system can enable music, dance, performance, spoken word, and nearly any kind of storytelling and performance imaginable, on the public stage of the city, a paragon of communication. It also acts as a revenue-generating urban infrastructure that links Allston with the music industry and can create funds to reinvest into the community and its residents (especially those with aspirations for performance).

The Arrow, programmed as The Street Corner, is actualized in a redeveloped Packard's Corner. The rich history of Packard's Corner is reimagined and re-presented to the public via a "Historical District Overlay," wherein new, unified, and reprogrammable "Historic" façades create a particular sense of place that revolves around the narrative of the corner's past, present, and future, juxtaposing and layering with a scaffolding that can also incorporate all the infinite histories that are yet to come.

Together, these ideal forms make up New Allston.

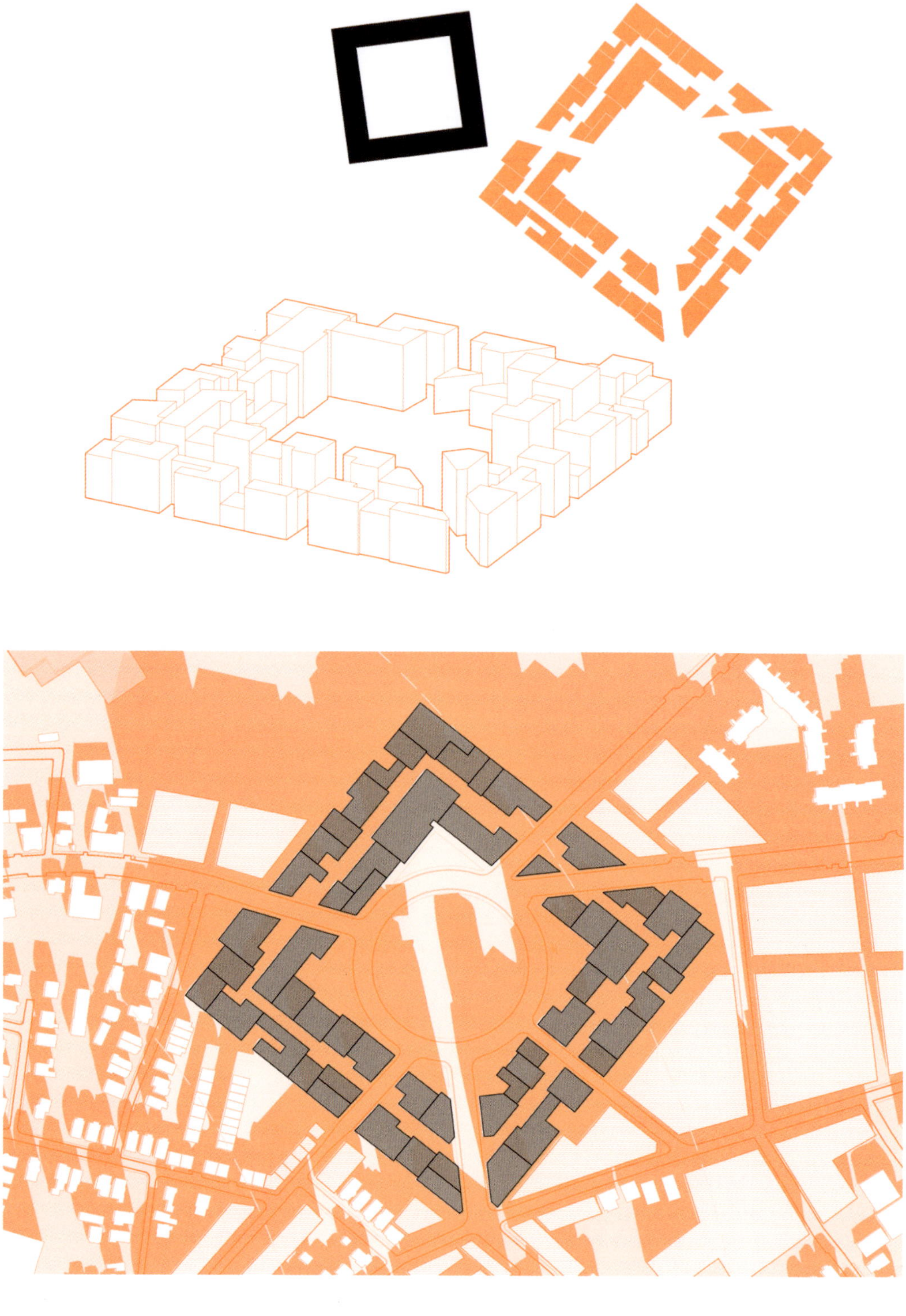

Top: Diagramming the ideal form of The Square. Bottom: The Square translated into The Classroom, a new development for Harvard's expansion. Source: author.

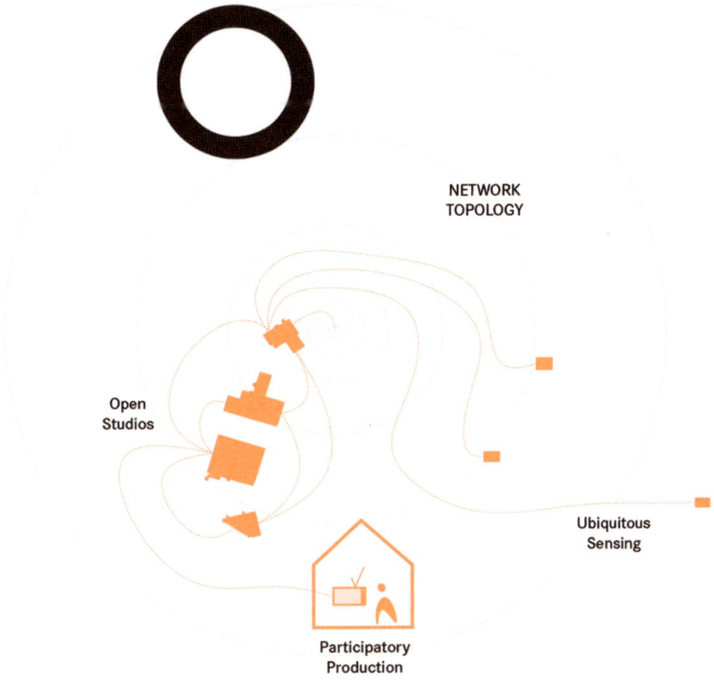

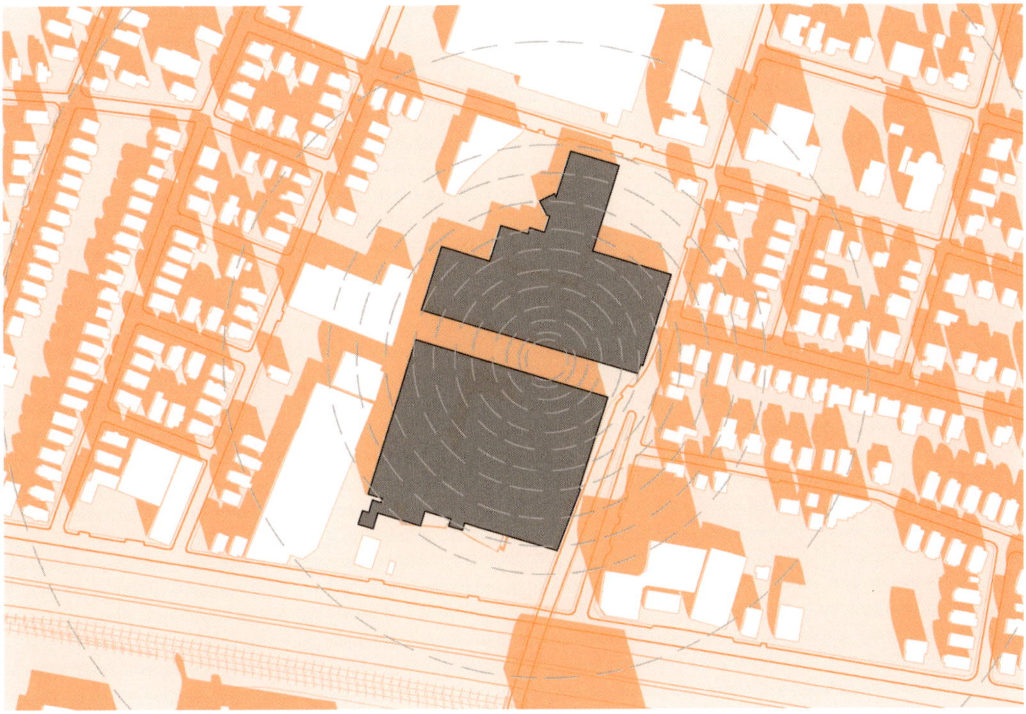

Top: Diagramming the ideal form of The Circle based on radio waves. Bottom: The Circle translated into The House, a home for the Media Circle Complex. Source: the author.

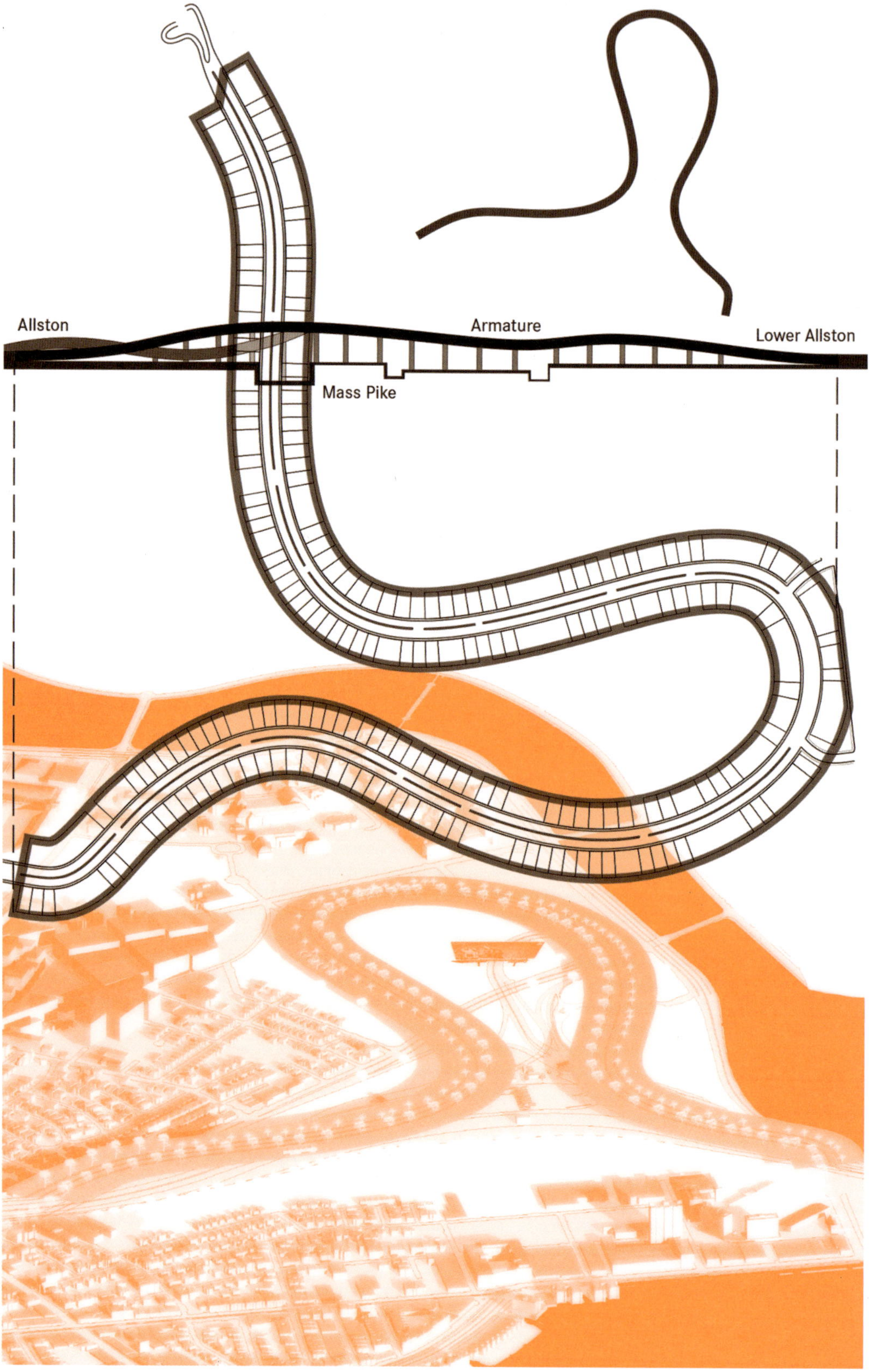
Allston
Armature
Lower Allston
Mass Pike

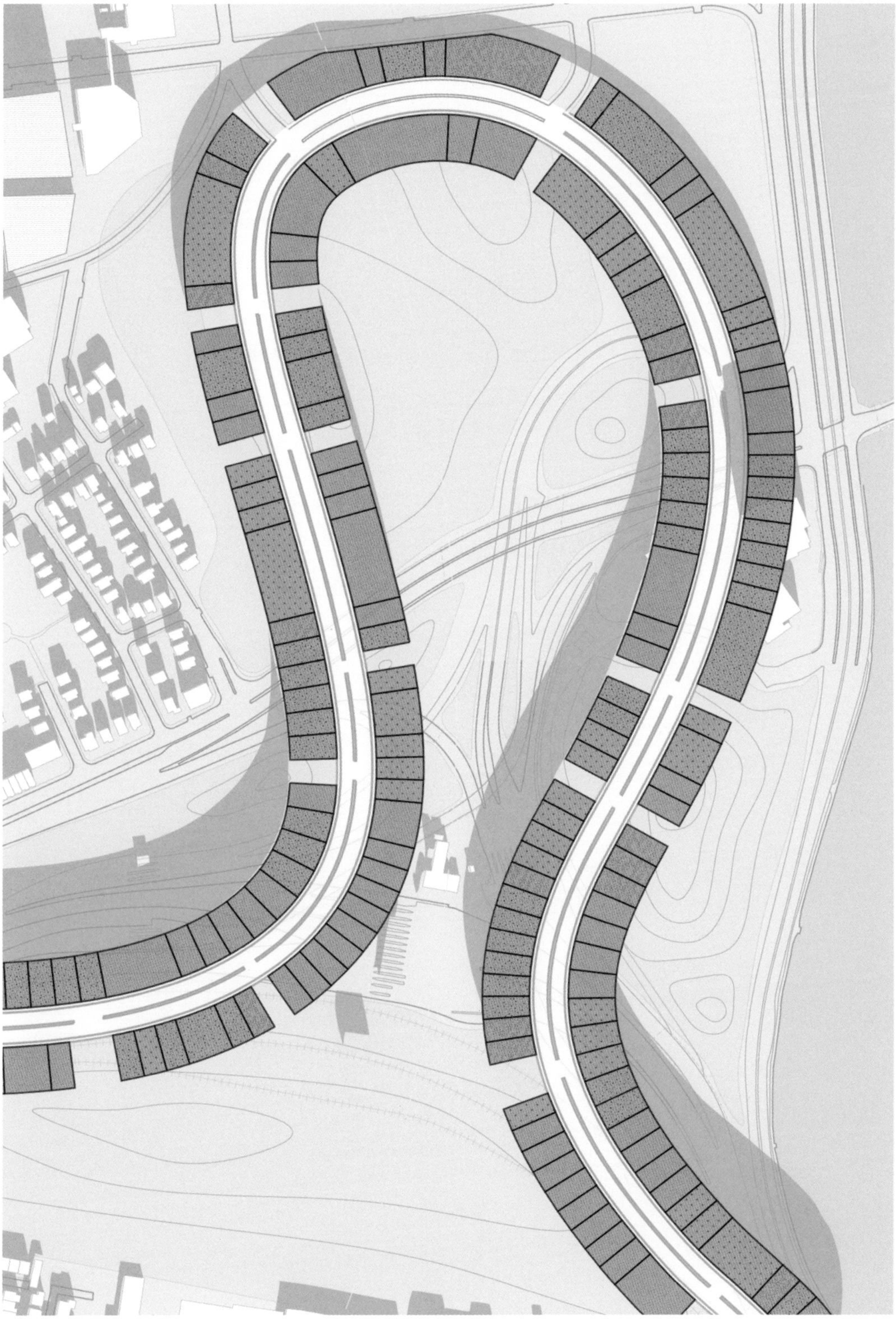

Opposite page: Diagram, plan, section, and rendering of the ideal form of The Curve translated into The Park, a new multi-use megaform. This page: Site plan for The Park. Source: author.

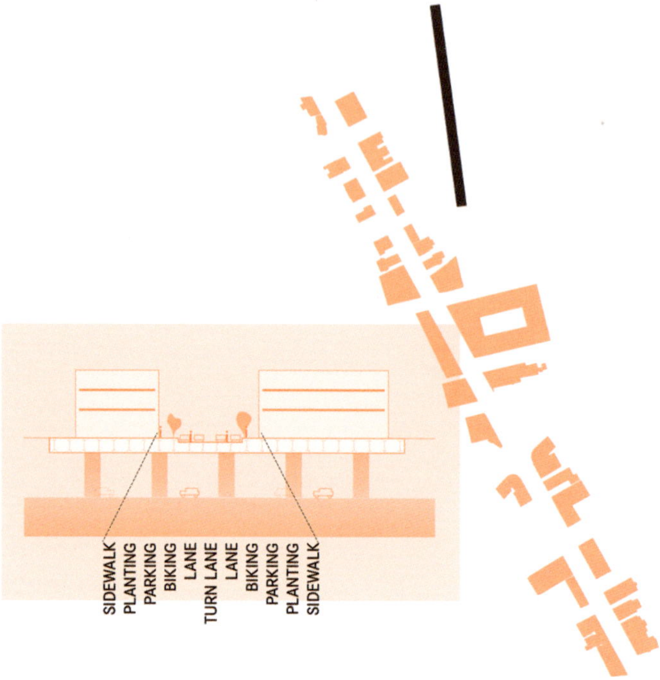

Top: Diagramming the ideal form of The Line, in an urban section. Bottom: Diagramming the ideal form of The Polyline, translated into The Stage, a sonic urban architecture made from hidden speakers known publicly as the Rock City Corridor. Opposite page: The Line translated into The Market, taking the form of the International Market Arcade. Also represented is a touchdown point for The Park and portions of the Rock City Corridor. Source: author.

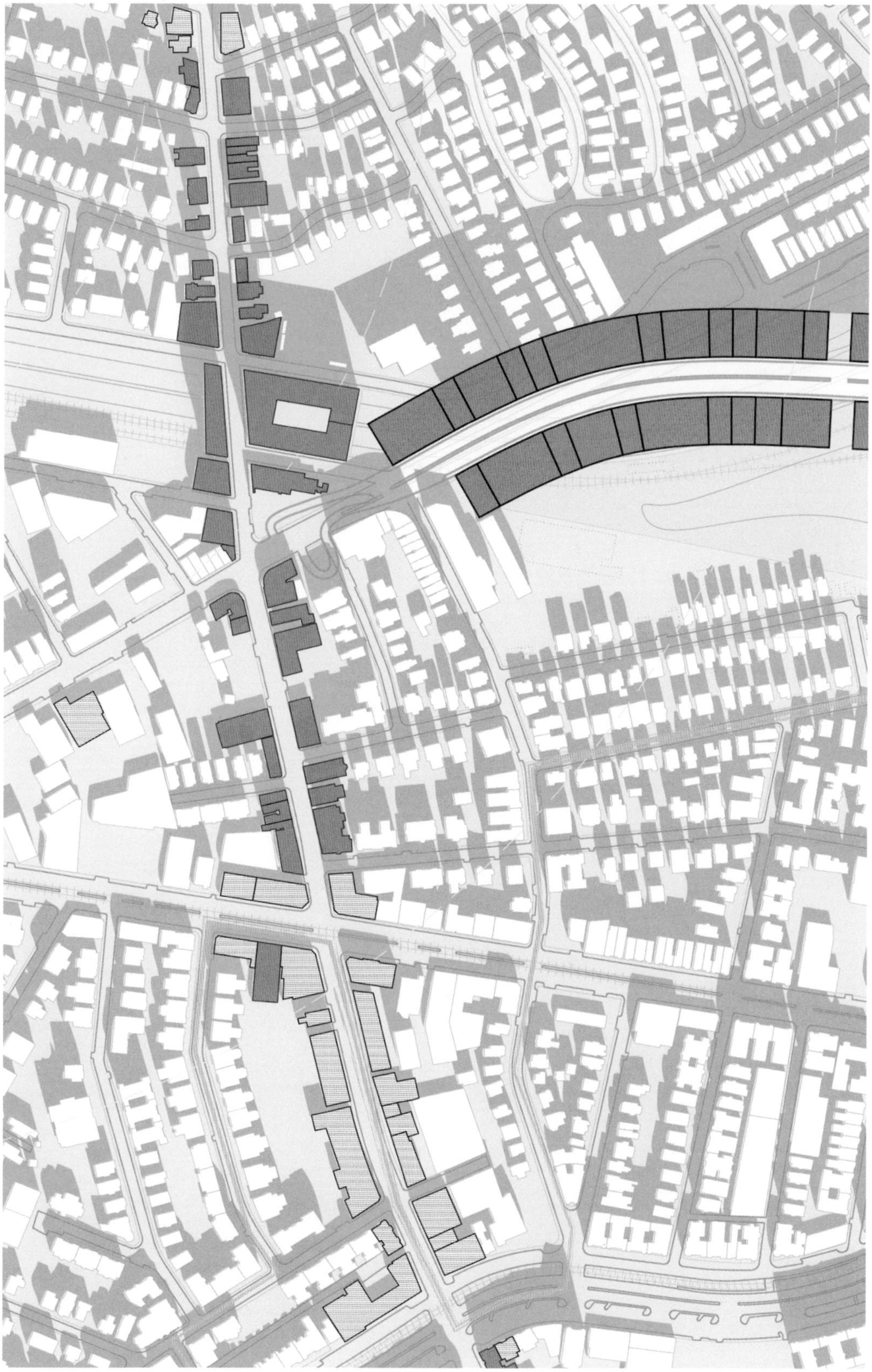

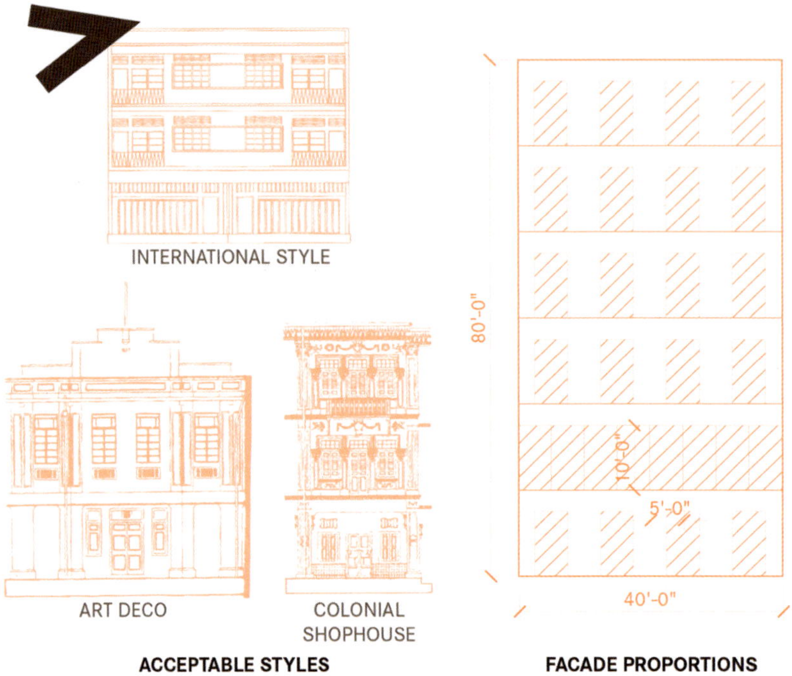

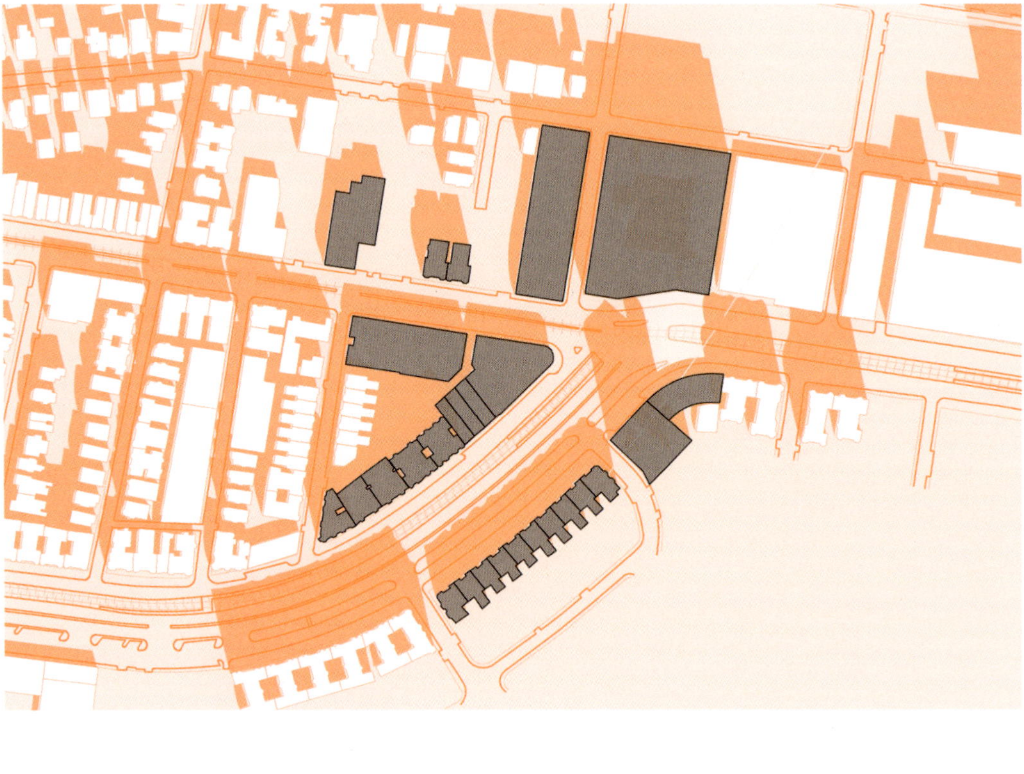

Top: Diagramming the ideal form of The Arrow, and the façade elements of its historical district overlay. Bottom: The Arrow translated into The Street Corner, known as Packard's Corner, based on the history programmed into its façade and contemporary use. Source: author.

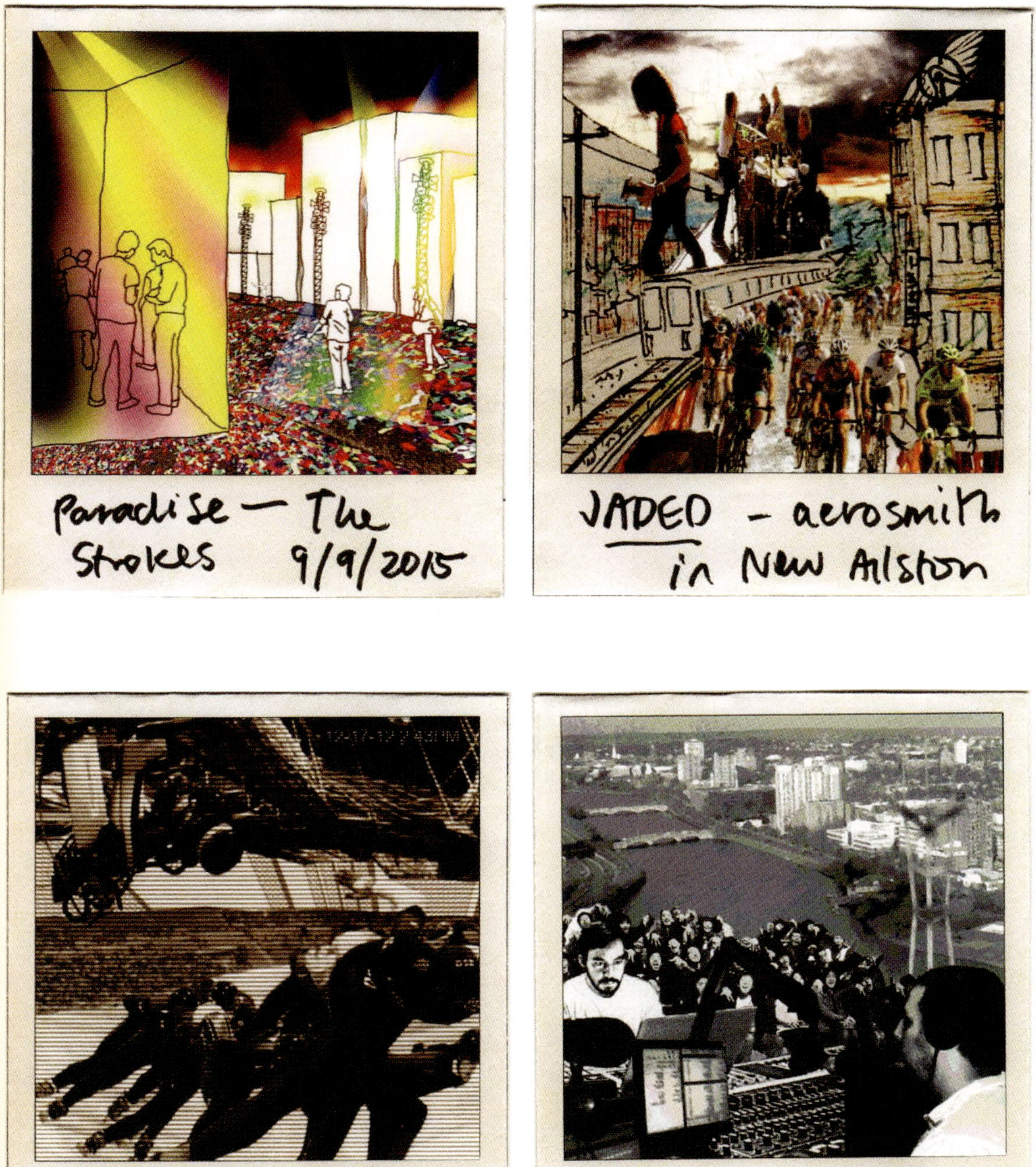

Polaroids of approximate translation in action. These particular Polaroids were created in collaboration with Galo Canizares, Edrie Ortega, Sarah Hirschman, and Chris Rhie. Source: author.

These particular Polaroids are the last of the Polaroids created for this project and were created in collaboration with Richard Ong, Jasmine Kwak, Brian Hoffer, and Beomki Lee. Source: author.

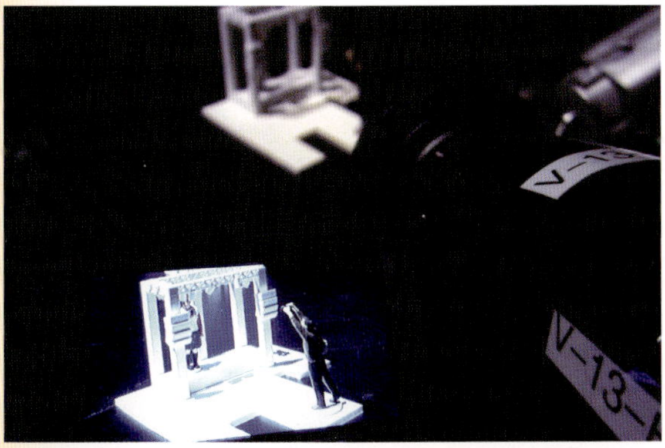

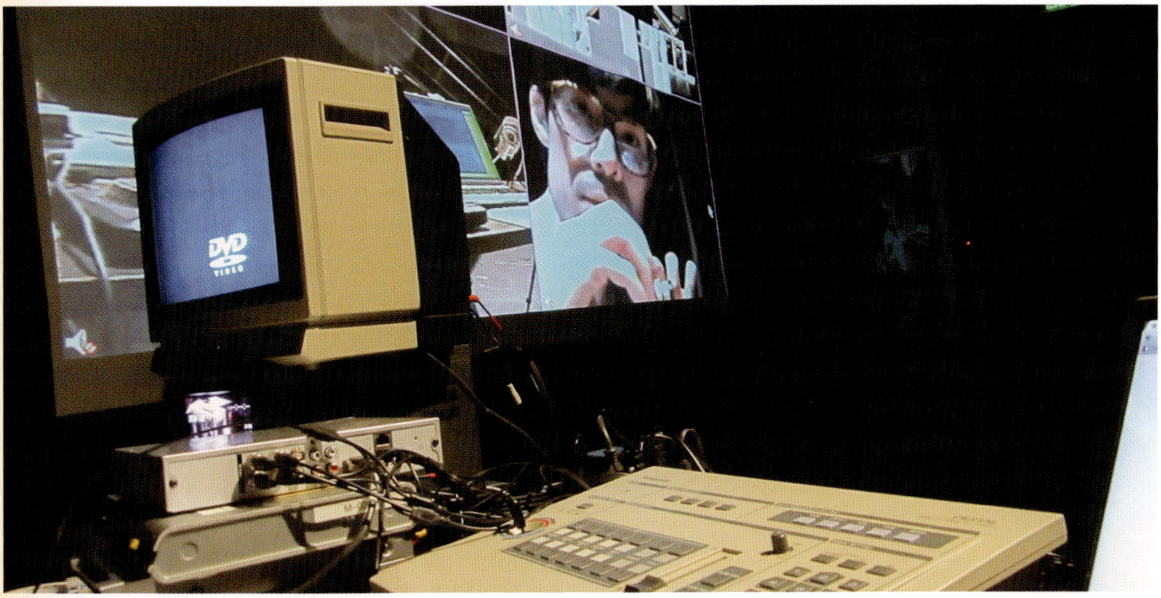

This page and next page: Interlude with behind the scenes photos of live model setup. In reading order: (1) live video feed with 3D printed model; (2) close-up of The Stage; (3) the author setting up video mixing equipment; (4) live mixing setup; (5) live mixing in action; (6–9) close-ups of The House, The Street Corner, The Classroom, and The Market; and (10) audience viewing of the live model in action. Source: author.

Chapter 7

Surrealization: A Live Model of Allston

In this final chapter, we will consider a fundamental element of urban design practice, and some tactics for accomplishing this practice: namely, that of representation. For all designers, the process of creating some imagined, ideal form is actually one of proposition. For some designers, they may create prototypes or even realize their designs (as new fabrication technologies increasingly allow), but for most, we create a vision for something that is to exist in the future, consider all the details and instructions necessary for its creation, and hand them off to those who will execute those instructions, be they a construction firm, a print shop, a software developer, or a factory. This is the process of design. But especially important for public design—as urban design typically is—are the forms of representation used to convey, explain, and engage a design with the public. In urban design, for example, you may need to develop technical plans to convey a design to an engineering firm, but you may also need to produce renderings and diagrams specifically for a public workshop.

Related to this, a critical yet often overlooked element in the practice of urban design is the question of narrative—narratives embedded in urban space that we can use in the process of understanding a site, narratives that we construct to make our urban designs better, or perhaps the narratives that we tell each other and to the public to enact new futures. We have discussed these narratives elsewhere in this book as place-embedded histories, understandings of the practical past, and the kinds of structures that exist for embedding narratives into themed and scripted spaces (as well as time-based media, such as film). Another place urban designers can learn about how to "design" narratives for urban space comes from art practice. In this chapter, we will explore how better understanding urban narratives can help us create more robust forms of urban design representations that integrate time, media, and narrative—and, in particular, through a process of "surrealization" into a medium I call the "live model."

Meta-narratives and Alter-histories

One art practice that we can learn from is Urbonas Studio. The interdisciplinary practice made up of Lithuanian artists Nomeda and Gediminas Urbonas, in their words, "deploys a methodology of organizational aesthetics to create complex participatory works that investigate urban environment, cultural and technological sphere and challenges of new climatic regimes."[1] In other words, they have demonstrated in their practice a penchant for drawing inspiration from organizational structures that set up working relationships between people, such as "the school" or "the laboratory," to drive participatory art projects on topics related to climate change, urbanism, technology, and political issues. Their work, driven by their own personal experiences, also often engages questions of the politics of the Cold War and a post-Cold War world that must still contend with the aftermath of that era.

In one such project from 2012, *Hearsay House*, Urbonas Studio, in collaboration with "Group 4.333" (a class of MIT students that I co-led), directed its focus towards the historic Höfði House in Reykjavík, Iceland, to craft an alternative historical narrative as an intervention for the Reykjavík Arts Festival. This architectural landmark bore witness to a momentous occasion: a meeting of then-U.S. President Ronald Reagan and the Soviet Union's President Mikhail Gorbachev in 1986, marking the beginning of the end of the Cold War. Through site-specific artistic interventions, *Hearsay House* brought together a network of artistic, scholarly, and community partners in Iceland to reenact a historical moment impossible to "accurately" replicate. Cameras, sensors, monitors, microphones, and other media were integrated into the house, drawing this network of partners in to impart pressure, breath, voice, motion, and other elements during a series of events, including a party, a knitting circle, and a tour. These traces were then translated and broadcast into a series of installations in the Reykjavík Art Museum, including projections, a weather balloon, and listening booths.

1 Nomeda Urbonas and Gediminas Urbonas, "Urbonas Studio," accessed March 14, 2024, https://nugu.lt/us/?p=1.

A knitting circle at the Höfði House in Iceland transmitting patterns through the laptop into an installation at the Reykjavik Art Museum as part of the Hearsay House project by Urbonas Studio with Group 4.333. Source: author.

A rotary phone in a bathroom at the Höfði House in Iceland transmitting voices into an installation at the Reykjavik Art Museum as part of the Hearsay House project by Urbonas Studio with Group 4.333. Source: author.

Translated media in the Reykjavik Art Museum as part of the Hearsay House project by Urbonas Studio with Group 4.333. Source: author.

While the material, technological, and participatory elements of the project were conceptually important, the narrative intervention that the work performed was equally critical. The multidisciplinary and multimodal piece explicitly referenced the site's history through photo and video documentation from the Cold War meeting, but also implicitly suggested speculative histories that could have been. For example, a rotary phone of the era was placed in the bathroom, purportedly the only bug-free zone in the house, according to some apocryphal tales, channeling in recordings made in the Reykjavík Art Museum and vice versa during the installation. In so doing, the piece reenacted and represented likely histories that spoke to the kind of human-scale micronarratives that convey the tense reality of that moment in time far better than a vast and abstract recounting of Cold War politics might have. I call this kind of art practice the construction of "alter-histories," intentionally constructed micronarratives that plausibly could be, a kind of retroactive science fiction.

Alter-histories are valuable in that they make the past real in such a way that it can inform our present and future. In grammar we might think of the unreal past, or the hypothetical past, while in literature or design thinking we often use counterfactuals—what if this had occurred, or supposing if this imaginary past was indeed our past. How would that impact what we think today? Though alter-histories are a shade different, rather than what-ifs, they instead present a structure for making often abstract and distant narratives of the past much more tangible, real, and affective. This is an alternative to supposing an extreme and playing that out—like designers Dunne and Raby suggest in their speculative design methodologies.[2] Here we are presented with something closer to what I discussed earlier in this volume as White's notion of the practical past: a close-enough approximation of history that is, in fact, even more productive for informing how we ought to live today and tomorrow, rather than the professional histories of historians that somehow feel still just beyond our reach.[3] Rather than the practical stories that we use in our day-to-day lives that White refers to, however, here instead we see stories that are intentionally constructed within the work of art to ground some kind of larger history and its lessons within imagined micronarratives of the past.

Another example, also with curiously similar Cold War resonances to *Hearsay House*, can be seen in the work of Swiss conceptual artist Christian Philipp Müller who, I argue, also often creates alter-histories as works of art within his practice. In his *Space Rendezvous* project for Manifesta 7 in 2008, he discovered a still-wrapped package of Apollo-Soyuz cigarettes at a tobacco factory during a preparatory site visit to Rovereto, Italy, where the biennale was to be held.[4] Apollo-Soyuz was a special brand of cigarette produced from 1975 to 1980 by Philip Morris to commemorate the Soviet-American space mission of the same name, featuring an image of the two spacecraft docked to one another. He also discovered during his site research that the Italian Futurist artist Fortunato Depero had designed a parade float for this same factory in 1936 that drew inspiration from tank mechanics and didn't look altogether dissimilar from the Apollo and Soyuz spacecraft.

2 Anthony Dunne and Fiona Raby, *Speculative Everything: Design, Fiction, and Social Dreaming* (Cambridge: MIT Press, 2013).

3 Hayden White, *The Practical Past* (Evanston: Northwestern University Press, 2014).

4 Christian Philipp Müller, "Space Rendezvous," accessed March 16, 2024, https://christianphilippmueller.ch/index/works/Space-Rendezvous.

A reenactment of a Futurist parade float, instead celebrating the Apollo-Soyuz space mission at the 2008 Manifesta in Roverto, Italy as part of Christian Philipp Müller's Space Rendezvous project. Source: Christian Philipp Müller.

For his project, Müller created a reenactment of Depero's parade float, complete with local participants wearing traditional clothing of that era, but in this case featuring a large-scale model of the Apollo-Soyuz spacecraft. He also installed a quasi-historical exhibition that featured historical imagery and video footage from Depero's parade in 1936, the Soviet-American mission in 1975, and the present-day parade in 2008, along with fabricated "historical" printed materials, and carefully protected ephemera such as the Apollo-Soyuz cigarettes.

Once again, these idiosyncratic and distant historical moments held important resonances for Müller and, in his estimation, also for locals and those inspired to participate in his project. Yet they were moments not deemed worth locating within the "grand narratives" of history, nor were they adequately documented to retroactively write "accurate" historical narratives. So, instead, Müller generated an alter-history as a work of art, constructing and designing his own narrative arcs that suited his purpose and, moreover, produced the kinds of tangible and affective experiences necessary to convey to his participants and audiences—and, perhaps, even himself—the importance and meaning of these curiously intersecting historical moments.

Designing and creating alter-histories embedded within a site-specific design can be a powerful way to enrich the affective qualities of a place. Urban designers can develop everyday narratives that plausibly fit into a place and its history, making real what otherwise might remain latent, abstract, or lacking in emotional resonance. Another way of thinking about these alter-histories comes from theories of history and historiography itself.

Jean-François Lyotard, in his 1979 book *The Postmodern Condition: A Report on Knowledge*, summarized the most widely cited pithy definition of postmodernism, which is that it is an "incredulity toward metanarratives."[5] By this, he meant that the "grand narratives" by which social belief and truth are structured, such as religion or science, had lost their totalizing power. Instead, he suggested that language games, at least in the Western context, had come to play a role as the barest essential collective meaning required for social relations—language games being essentially the same as the kinds of deconstruction operations I discuss earlier in this book.

Later in his volume, Lyotard suggests that "popular narrative pragmatics" are a kind of self-legitimating practice that non-Western cultures use in lieu of metanarratives—though, of course, this Eurocentric view ignores that fact that this kind of storytelling is and always has been used by humans regardless of historical period or geography, including in "the West."[6] In any case, these "popular narrative pragmatics" are what others, including Fredric Jameson in his forward to Lyotard's volume, have referred to as "small narratives" and what I, along with others, have called "micronarratives."[7] I suggest that these are very much in line with the kinds of narratives that are useful for urban designers to develop and integrate into proposals and representations for urban space, of which alter-histories might be one fairly sophisticated version.

If we consider the postmodern move toward the rejection of metanarratives as a kind of deconstruction, at least within the context of critical theory, then the construction of alter-histories and micronarratives can be a strategy toward reconstruction—and, as I've discussed earlier, the more the merrier! A move toward "approaching infinity" can build or at least reveal what metanarrative may yet remain in our midst. (And, indeed, Jameson also suggests that metanarratives may not have fully disappeared but simply moved "underground.")[8]

Indeed, Daniel Punday, in his book *Narrative after Deconstruction*, grapples with precisely that, pointing out, however, the limitations of narrative as a salve for a deconstructed world. He suggests that they either return to the same totalizing tendencies of metanarratives thus demanding new kinds of deconstruction, or they center a visibility of the narrator's positionality (not entirely a bad thing) that can then limit the narrative's social power to a kind of tentative localism.[9]

5 Jean-François Lyotard, *The Postmodern Condition: A Report on Knowledge* (Minneapolis: University of Minnesota Press, 1984 [1979]), xxiv.

6 Ibid., 23.

7 Ibid., xi.

8 Ibid., xii.

9 Daniel Punday, *Narrative after Deconstruction* (Albany: SUNY Press, 2002).

Further, and perhaps more interesting for our purposes, Punday charts the parallels between post-deconstruction narrative and the rise in theories of materialism: that just as narrative is being deployed in new ways to ground and reconstruct a seemingly endless self-referential system of signs that came from the linguistic turn and deconstruction, so too is materiality being deployed to identify, understand, ground, and intervene in the dynamic relationships between subject and object. In other words, intervening in the materiality of our world—be it altering power structures that govern human relationships, or undertaking new forms of urban design that invite, say, the non-human beings in our midst to take on new subjectivities—is its own kind of narrative-based reconstruction. We can do this with micronarratives, a reminder that the "smallest" things can be the most powerful.

If we return to our example of New Allston, we can see how select interventions in material and narrative space can transform this place for the better—and do so without the demands for a tabula rasa erasure so lauded by urban design interventions of the grand narrative era of modernism (take Le Corbusier's Ville Contemporaine as the ur-example). And if we seek out an approach toward infinity, we need not center any one narrative: instead, a multitude of micronarratives actually serves us better. In the words of adrienne maree brown, "small is all."[10]

10 adrienne maree brown, *Emergent Strategy: Shaping Change, Shaping Worlds* (Chico: AK Press, 2017), 41.

Where these micronarratives can be used by urban designers as a design tool in their own right—consider, for example, the urban histories reimagined and deployed as material interventions in space in New Allston—they can also be understood as a form of representation of the designed urban plan. To continue our example, as a means of conveying the reality presented by New Allston, the conventional tool of digital rendering has been replaced with a participatory process involving readers rather than just designers. Dozens of designers not associated with creating or formulating the project were presented with it as a work-in-progress and asked to construct their own micronarrative of a moment in the design in the form of a Polaroid photo—these are the images in the interludes between the earlier chapters of this book.

This approach invited individuals to immerse themselves in the plan and associated documents, which provide a broad yet fuzzy image of the project's totality (just as any end user of a designed space would experience) and subsequently produce a small image of what they perceive in the design and, in particular, what resonated with them. These "Polaroids" provide both individual experiences as parts and yet also an aggregate image that is far more accurate and total than a conventional rendering despite—and due to—their fractured, cloudy presentation. Each image is a bit of narrative truth, different though they may be, collectively coming to better represent an urban place—and all its layers of interpretive meaning—than any one totalizing image could. The old parable of the blind men and the elephant come to mind, each of us struggling to identify reality on our own when, really, a kind of collectivity is necessary.

Surrealization: Manipulating Urban Media

In the introductory manifesto to this volume, I propose the potential of surrealism as a method for taking the popular—theme parks included—and unearthing the subversive, subconscious, and sublime potential latent within it. In André Breton's lecture, "Situation of the Surrealist Object," he points out the "paranoiac-critical" method used by Salvador Dalí to "penetrate the deepest layers of the mental."[11] Dalí, for his part, defines the process as "a spontaneous method of irrational knowledge based on the critical and systemic objectification of delirious associations and interpretations." In other words, to see the world like a paranoiac offers new connections and patterns to our field of vision, even if they may not be there, while to see that world like a critic can systematically boil down these "associations and interpretations" to a point where they become something like knowledge.[12]

This is, in fact, the eponymous method for Rem Koolhaas's *Delirious New York*, a city based on a kind of paranoiac-critical structure where new things are invented by dream-like juxtapositions enabled by the Manhattan grid and all its congestion.[13] And of course, I offer the modest strip mall as a kind of paranoiac-critical structure for delightfully unexpected new possibilities the world over. Koolhaas, in fact, is in large part inspired by "anti-constructionalist" Dalí's move to New York and subsequent demonization of "constructionalist" Le Corbusier who represents in many ways the opposite of the paranoiac-critical method, offering instead the concrete—both literally and conceptually.[14]

11 André Breton, *Manifestoes of Surrealism* (Ann Arbor, MI: University of Michigan Press, 1969), 274.

12 Ibid.

13 Rem Koolhaas, *Delirious New York: A Retroactive Manifesto for Manhattan* (New York: The Monacelli Press, 1997).

14 Simon Weir, "Salvador Dalí in Rem Koolhaas' Delirious New York," *The Journal of Architecture* 27, no. 2–3 (2022): 398–419, https://doi.org/10.1080/13602365.2022.2106580.

Philippe Halsman's photograph of Salvador Dalí titled "Dali Atomicus" (1948), showing the paranoiac-critical mind at work. Source: Library of Congress, LC-DIG-ppmsca-09633.

For the urban designer, this produces several useful outcomes. First, the paranoiac-critical is a method of narrative construction, as the subconscious mind creates patterns and the conscious mind constructs stories to explain those patterns. Second, and moreover, the paranoiac-critical mind produces a kind of hyperactive analysis of urban spaces and narratives such that one can cycle through and address all the possible imaginaries, criticisms, hopes, and fears that are held by that very public with whom you are trying to engage. These are often layered and conflicting with one another, demanding a kind of surreal juxtaposition to accommodate them all.

Returning again to the work of Iris Marion Young and her notion of a "politics of difference," urban designs that can accommodate for these conflicting "surrealities" require an "unoppressive openness."[15] In her writings, Young emphasizes the importance of recognizing and engaging with diverse perspectives and experiences to foster understanding and solidarity across various social and cultural divides. Her work also underscores the role of narrative and communication in acknowledging the existence of others' experiences and viewpoints.[16] This aligns with the idea of using surrealism as a means to bridge differences by creating alternative, imaginative realities that welcome and invite audiences to explore and understand various perspectives including but also that go beyond their own. The technique of the "live model" described later in this chapter echoes Young's emphasis on narratives and interactions that go beyond mere intellectual coherence, fostering immersive experiences that engage our entire sensorium.

All of this to say, surrealism offers untapped tools and techniques for altering the status quo beyond the confines and goals of the Surrealist project itself. While it was an avant-garde project with aims to solve social issues and alter power structures, the Surrealists went the way of many movements as its members began to disagree in unproductive ways, became interested in other projects, or simply died, as in the case of the de facto, and perhaps overly quarrelsome, leader of the Surrealists, Breton, whose death is often cited as the end of the movement.

Regardless, its ideas and practices live on: the Surrealists championed the primacy of dreams, the unconscious mind, and other forms of ignored reality as a means of comprehending and intervening in the world around us. In an age where the dream of capital accumulation has become totalizing, the only means of escape is to dream of something else, of an alternative reality—a practice that I am proposing for urban design as "surrealization." This practice, while it can be used during the process of urban design, is especially useful in the final stages of a project where you must engage and integrate a public into the design process, produce representations that can convey the intentions of a design at its essence, and allow for input and co-creation with and from this public. This is at least one possible process for taking surrealist practices and using them to realize or improve an urban design project.

15 Iris Marion Young, "The Ideal of Community and the Politics of Difference," *Social Theory and Practice* 12, no. 1 (1986): 1–26. See also: Iris Marion Young, *Inclusion and Democracy* (Oxford: Oxford University Press, 2002).

16 Ibid.

Let's return again to this paradox of public design that I mentioned earlier in this chapter: urban designers must undertake two parallel paths of creation which are, in fact, often conflated or undifferentiated, and which also recursively influential on one another. First, creating an actual technical design through to be actualized by professionals, and second, creating representations of that design for public consumption and engagement. Media scholar Shannon Mattern picks apart some of these threads in her analysis of the "morphological resonance between writing, an integral political-economic and cultural media infrastructure, and the shape of the city itself":[17]

"The architects of the ancient world," architect Mario Carpo suggests, "would have drawn up their actual project designs only at the building site and while the works were in full swing. The drawings that they made were working plans, often done at full scale"—in other words, written directly on the building site. The earth was their substrate. . . . Other genres of architectural thought—rules, theory, standards, etc.—likewise took form on different media substrates: manuscripts, printed books, oral address. These formats of communication shaped the advice authors dispensed, which in turn shaped the built environment their readers created. Clay tablets and scrolls shaped architectural thought, which in turn informed the arrangement of bricks and stones. These texts thus mediated the translation of mud and stone into urban form—a form that both embodied an ideology and created a platform for a society to perform its politics.[18]

17 Shannon Mattern, *Code and Clay, Data and Dirt: Five Thousand Years of Urban Media* (Minneapolis: University of Minnesota Press, 2017), 100.

18 Ibid., 101.

Recipe for a Live Model

Scholars have noted the visual bias of urban design, privileging the plan and other drawings that represent and create built form over other media that might better convey other sensory modalities experienced in the city, such as sound and smell.[19] Architecture and urban design focuses on space and, as such, they are inherently experiential, unlike other kinds of design, such as graphic design, which is intended to be visual-centric. Whole segments of the human sensorium thus go overlooked in conventional architectural and urban design practice. Mattern, again writing on urban media and focusing in particular on the human voice and on soundscapes in general within the city, describes the centrality of these senses, so overlooked in professionalized urban design practice:

> *[The voice] has always been merely one in a larger sonic, visual, textural, and performative symphony of urban mediation. The way we hear urban voices is informed by this broader urban "sensory economy," by our cultural and historical and spatial contexts, by our own situational or generational "audile techniques."*[20]

19 Raymond Lucas and Ombretta Romice, "Representing Sensory Experience in Urban Design," *Design Principles and Practices* 2, no. 4 (2008): 83–94, https://doi.org/10.18848/1833-1874/CGP/v02i04/37579.

20 Mattern, *Code and Clay, Data and Dirt*, 131.

My own experience of the city—"the city" being a kind of hypernym for a multitude of places, a combinatory and delirious memoryscape of my own making—hardly aligns with the professionalized representations used for it within urban planning and design. The things that I love about the city, the reasons why I made this infinitely complex cultural object the focus of my intellectual life, have everything to do with the fundamental aspects of human experience: relationships between people, between people and space, relationships that exist in temporal space, dynamic relationships in which the unexpected occurs. The interplay, in short, between event, people, and place that make up the narratives of our lives.

In other words, our static, typically two-dimensional representations of urban spaces and places, the plans, the renderings, the diagrams of proposals for the future of our cities, representations so often devoid of people within them—and so often pale, colorless people of a comfortable upper-middle class when they do appear—simply do not capture or show what makes a city a city. And, in turn, they are thus inadequate for a process of urban design that includes those fundamental elements that make the city so special: elements of time, experience, mediation, chance, relationship, interaction, and narrative.

Artist Vincent Chong mid-performance at QNA, a party co-organized by the author that exemplifies the kind of urban experience not represented in professionalized design representation. Source: author.

I take inspiration from McKenzie Wark's recent work on raves and nightlife as capturing something essential about urban experience. While her work isn't on the urban, per se, the sociality found within rave and nightlife spaces is instructive, showing us how social spaces—and cities as the ur-formation of a social space—are not fixed designs with carefully scripted behaviors that unfold within them but, rather, creative oppositions to the built environment. She describes that "chasing street raves is a way to rediscover the city, to find the texture of neglected junkspace" with ravers acting as a kind of contemporary anti-flaneur, walking through the city to inscribe it and reconstruct social space.[21] Or perhaps their activities are of a hyperconscious Situationist dérive, the uncovering not only of latent psychogeographies of the city, but also as a means of constructing new space out of the urban and spatial detritus of late capitalism—what Koolhaas has called, in a piece that is his own kind of surrealist automatism, "the residue mankind leaves on the planet"[22] and what Wark defines thus:

junkspace *Urban ambiences that hover between decaying forms of usage and novel potentials. Where a city's tendencies of coherent spatial organization fail. Good locations for constructed situations but inevitably prey to style extraction.*[23]

21 McKenzie Wark, *Raving* (Durham: Duke University Press, 2023), 26.

22 Rem Koolhaas, "Junkspace," *October* 100 (2002): 175–190, https://doi.org/10.1162/016228702320218457.

23 Wark, *Raving*, 92.

Implicitly, much of what architects and urban designers create, then, is junkspace. Superblock malls, privately-owned public spaces, airport plans. And the real essence of the city, then, is not necessarily enabled or encouraged by urban design but instead unfolds in opposition to urban design. New forms of urban design practice and representation can allow us to, at the very least, consider these oppositions and, ideally, reduce friction so that new, perhaps even entirely unplanned and unexpected forms of urban life can emerge. They can allow us to play out scenarios, to role play possibilities, to give something to work off of rather than in opposition to. Wark goes on to lay out some of these tensions:

I'm not the only one who came to Brooklyn from all over because it seemed to be a great machine for producing styles of life. To drift the streets, unknown to everyone. A stranger among strangers. At least on a good day. But there's what H calls the queer tax to pay. We have to gather here to feel alive, relatively safe, among our people, but we pay for it. . . . For queer and trans people, particularly if they aren't white, Brooklyn is still not any kind of home. Which is why there's nightlife. Another city for another life, but already immanent to this city, in its shadows.[24]

24 Ibid., 58.

The idea that the city would be "a great machine for producing styles of life" echoes the modernist aspirations of early urban designers like Le Corbusier who saw streets, open spaces, and buildings as components that enabled a humming-along modern life—Kevin Lynch described the city as "a practical machine" and Harvey Molotch described the city as "a growth machine."[25] But here Wark points out the limits of this imaginary, noting the disillusionment that comes with holding this aspiration only to find that living as a part in a machine is "not any kind of home," but that the recuperative possibility of nightlife offers a kind of human-centric urban space based on experience, intimacy, "to feel alive." Importantly, she points out that this city of the night is, like in China Miéville novel *The City & the City*, located contiguously with the planned city's daytime geography, it is "immanent" and "in its shadows."

What would an urban design practice and form of representation be that could consider and convey these shadow cities so important for our experience of urban life? How can elements of shared experience, collectivity, and serendipity—elements invisible within the static plan—come to the fore of urban representation? What medium affords time, narrative, and chance, affords us the opportunity to collectively dream new dreams? Here I offer the live model as one proposition toward this end, a live-mixed and multi-modal form of urban representation that, in fact, draws some of the same technologies from the rave and from nightlife: namely, DJ decks, VJ systems, live mixing, and audio-video media.

The live model is a structure for a new form of architectural and urban design representation. Conventional means of orthographic projection drawings, static models, and even pre-recorded fly-through or other demonstrative videos simply do not have the wherewithal to convey the contents of contemporary reality. To understand reality—and to understand the proposed alternative realities that design offers—we must communicate mediation, psycho-perception, and, above all, time. The live model, albeit in nascent form, offers a means to convey these elements which are as important as, or more important to, a design than formal or material properties. Critically, physical models within the live model are not construed as totalities but, rather, open-

25 Kevin Lynch, *A Theory of Good City Form* (Cambridge: MIT Press, 1981); Harvey Molotch, "The City as a Growth Machine: Toward a Political Economy of Place," *American Journal of Sociology* 82, no. 2 (1976): 309–332, https://doi.org/10.1086/226311.

ended, extensible, and discursive canvases which offer a living structure, allowing for improvisation, unexpected change, and outside influences.

At the heart of the live model is a collection of multimedia elements, governed by a script that acts much in the same way as a jazz composition: highly structured to allow for infinite unpredictable outcomes. A live video feed captures a physical model in real time; audio clips, from ambient urban noises to curated soundtracks, are layered to create an auditory landscape. Stock and original photos and videos, interspersed with curated movie clips, are projected onto the live video feed of the physical model through video mixing. These elements, when combined, transcend their individual identities. They intermingle, interact, and fuse to create a rich, immersive experience. With multiple people working the live model, moving the physical model pieces, mixing the audio and video, it becomes a dynamic entity, responding, evolving, and narrating stories on the fly. The live model isn't just a representation—it's a sensory journey that aims to encapsulate the multifaceted and unpredictable experience of city life.

I tested this live model technique as a way to convey and surrealize the urban design for New Allston. In the setup, live-feed video cameras surround segments of a model. Six white "game pieces" comprise the model, each a 3-dimensional printed architectural structure with different formal and spatial properties, with a balance of the generic, the abstract, and the specific. Libraries of clips from architecturally significant movies, quotes from literature, sounds (both real and constructed), music, and so on, await use. As the "model jockey" moves the pieces of the model in and out of the camera's frame, they simultaneously mix sound and visual content on their white surfaces, transforming a collection of bits and pieces into a total, immersive reality. The resulting media is something of a hybrid between a live performance and an audio-video broadcast. The video stills in the interlude after this chapter show at least a fragment of the mixed video portion of the surrealization of Allston, capturing some of the micronarratives imagined and embedded into this representation. As in the surrealist technique, the outcome is not an entirely straightforward, intellectually coherent narrative but, rather, an immersive narrative that requires the audience to project upon it their own multilayered and at times unconscious meanings—a new kind of projective drawing, indeed.

In addition to providing a communicative mode of representation, the live model also acts like other forms of representation: as a design tool. In planning, synthesizing, timing, and testing the live model, a designer will develop a greater degree of comprehension of how such media and narratives will unfold in real space. Indeed, the live model provides a critical and much-needed means to design for what is fast becoming the reality of designed space: based on media, narrative, and experience. But my hope is that through approximate translation from city to design and then into live model, we can collectively dream new dreams; we can create, in the words of Wark, another city for another life, uncover the life waiting to be lived that is right there, immanent in this place, but only hidden just so, in its shadows.[26]

26 There are a set of practices one can take—approximate translation among them—that I suggest can help you "rehearse" for the future, a future that operates much like Wark's "another city," immanent within our present and waiting to burst out. I call these practices "immanent speculation": Jonathan Jae-an Crisman, "Practicing the Future: Exercises in Immanent Speculation," *Boom: A Journal of California* 6, no. 3 (2016): 25–31, https://doi.org/10.1525/boom.2016.6.3.25.

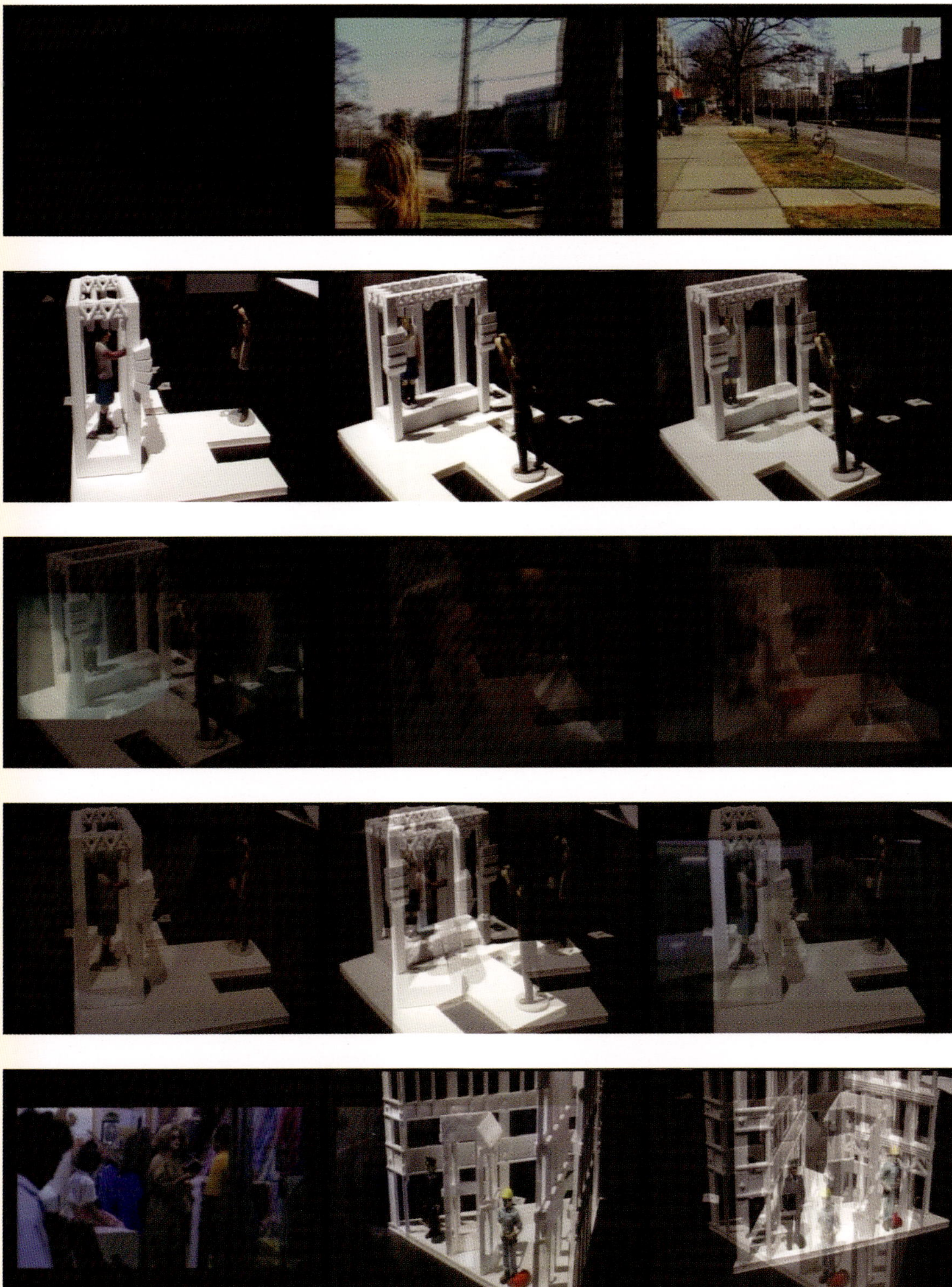

This page and next three pages: Interlude. Video stills from the live model surrealization of New Allston, discussed in the previous chapter. Source: author.

Police Pursuit

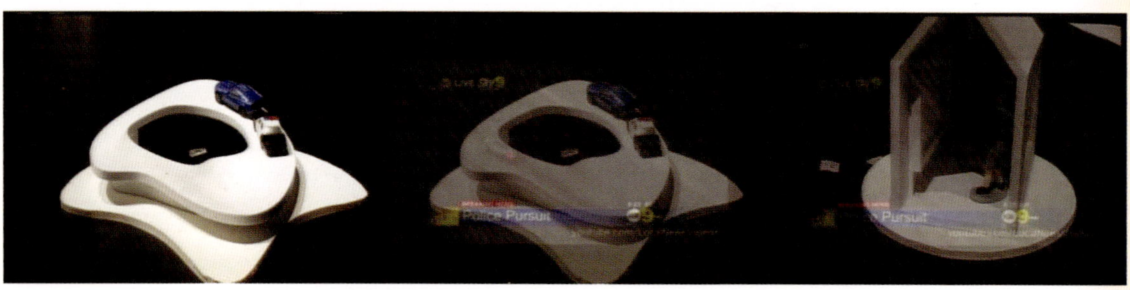
Police Pursuit

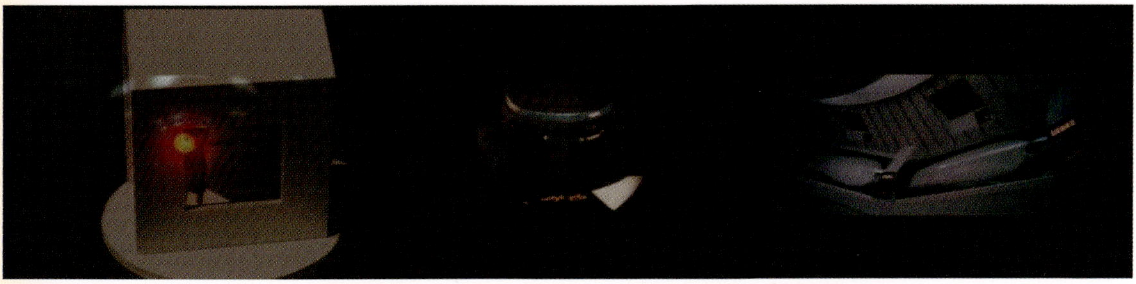

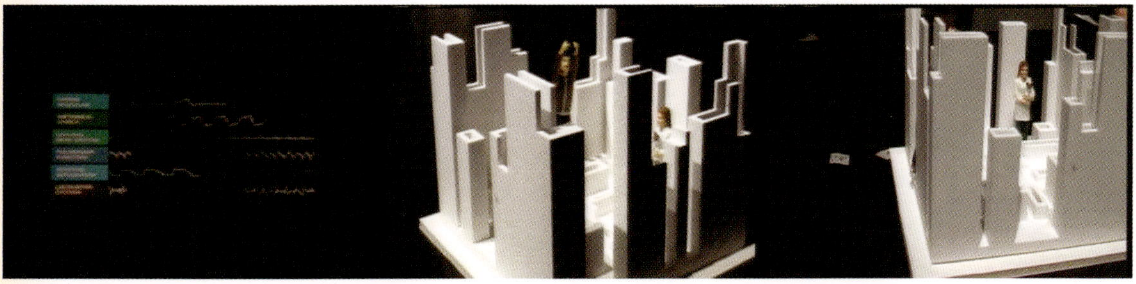

"...the machine!...
Someone has to stay
at the machine!"
"Someone will stay
at the machine..."
"ME"

Chapter 8

Conclusion: Approximate Translation as Urban Design

Let's revisit how we got here, recap our journey for a moment, think of all the places that we've been. In one sense, we drove down Alvarado Street in Los Angeles, California, stopped through Disneyland and Singapore. We've popped—pun intended—through London (the Whitechapel Gallery), returned once again to Los Angeles (MOCA), and made a quick stop through Nashville (the Parthenon). We've ultimately landed in Boston where we've spent a good deal of time in Allston. We've stopped over in Dresden, Rome, and Chicago (the World's Columbian Exposition), before going on a wholesale theme park voyage, seeing Vauxhall Gardens in London, Steeplechase Park in Brooklyn, Pacific Ocean Park in Santa Monica, Idora Park in Youngstown, Hersheypark in Hershey, Six Flags Over Texas in Arlington, all before returning once again to Disneyland, both in Southern California and in Orlando, Florida. We've spent some time in Hong

Kong, and in particular Penny's Bay on Lantau Island, building Allstonland, and compared and contrasted delirious urbanism in Manhattan's street grid and Los Angeles's strip malls (considering, for example, the extremes between Gehry's Walt Disney Concert Hall—Disney strikes again—and Kamnitzer's Promenade Plaza). We have seen non-extant futures and pasts for Paris (Eisenman's proposal for Parc de la Villette), Alexandria (the demolished Masrah Al Salam), and Tokyo (Tange's 1960 Plan, among other megaform sites), and also taken a look at Iceland (the Höfði House) and Italy (the Rovereto tobacco factory), before settling down, once and for all, in Allston once again.

Another way of recapping our journey is conceptual. We have considered how ideas from media studies might apply to architecture and urban design, giving us the possibility for an urban massage, a salve for out times where wicked problems make our cities knotty and tense. Despite well-worn critiques, mediated cities and spaces can be perhaps no better understood than through examination and analysis of theme parks—and perhaps their opposite, the generic city. And the influence of artistic movements, including Pop and Surrealism, are also productive vehicles for understanding not only mediated cities, but new strategies for intervening in them. We've considered notions of place-embedded history and the kinds of practical history that can inform urban design that stand distinct from the professionalized histories that often dominate. Once again, theme parks surface here, suggesting an alternative, practical history of urban design that is more scripted space and less CIAM. We unpacked narrative into its constituent parts, focusing on defamiliarization, considering how it can be used in urban design. And we have approached infinity, examining the similarities between the deliriousness of Manhattan's street grid and Los Angeles's strip malls—found in their "no style" approach to design. We have revisited Plato, no less, reflecting on his solids and forms and, subsequently, to megaforms to strategize on how to reconstruct that which has been left deconstructed by deconstructivists and their linguistic turn. And, finally, we looked at alter-histories in art practices along with surrealism and nightlife to understand how we might attempt to construct new forms of urban representation.

Related to this conceptual journey is a kind of voyage of the minds. Here I recount only a fraction of the all the people, artists, scholars, designers, and thinkers that have populated these pages. Artists: André Breton and Salvador Dalí (the Surrealists), Pipilotti Rist, Nomeda and Gediminas Urbonas, and Christian Philipp Müller (the contemporaries and the alter-historians), and Fortunato Depero (the futurist). Theorists and thinkers: Marshall McLuhan and Shannon Mattern (media), Michel de Certeau and Iris Marion Young (urban life—that is to say, everyday life for diverse people in the public sphere), Hayden White and Jean-François Lyotard (narratives and metanarratives), Jacques Derrida (deconstruction), Proclus and Plato (ideal forms), Bertold Brecht and Viktor Shklovsky (estrangement and defamiliarization, respectively), and McKenzie Wark (nightlife, that city within a city). Theme park creators and critiquers: Cornelius Tilyou (Steeplechase), Angus Wynne (Six Flags), Walt Disney (you know this one), Norman Klein, Scott Lukas, and Michael Sorkin. Our historical figures of Allston: Washington Allston, Alexander Graham Bell, Helen Keller, Alvan Tufts Fuller, and of course, Aerosmith. And architects and architectural scholars: Giambattista Nolli (of the eponymous map), Le Corbusier (of CIAM fame), Kenzo Tange and Kenneth Frampton (megaform maker and later critic), Peter Eisenman (of deconstructivism, among other things), Frank Gehry and Peter Kamnitzer (dueling across Hope in Downtown LA), Mark Jarzombek (of urban heterology), and Rem Koolhaas (of perhaps too many influences; why does this mind hold such monopolistic sway over architectural thinking of a particular era—though perhaps the same can be said of Le Corb).

Another path: at the heart of this volume is the journey that we foist upon Allston, an everyday neighborhood in Boston, Massachusetts. We take Allston through a conventional urban design process involving consideration of network and figure-ground analysis, creating new networks that connect lost pathways and filling in its plan with needed uses. We use "displacement" to take Allston out of Allston and drop it into Hong Kong, using design strategies from theme parks including deployment of place-embedded histories, to create Allstonland. We use "replacement" with theories of ideal forms to create New Allston, creating The Circle, The Square, The Line, The Curve, The Arrow, and The Polyline. And we surrealize New Allston in the form of a "live model," using techniques of micronarrative, alter-history, time-based multi-sensorial media, and nightlife, to create a new, experiential form of urban representation. This overall process of urban design cum art project acts as a speculative experiment through which we can demonstrate, test, and examine all of these proposed new practices for use by urban designers.

The path you take likely depends on where you began: as a scholar, as an urban designer, or as a curious reader without a connection to the professional spaces of urbanism? But, perhaps at this point, to re-read along a different path might lead to new insights and revelations: approximate translation can offer us all something distinct; it is many things.

Approximate Translation: A Cipher

Approximate translation is more a classification that can tie many ideas together than any one theory, concept, or practice on its own. It is the process of transformation, creation, and discovery that occurs when one translates something from one language, space, or medium to another. As Homi Bhabha, citing Walter Benjamin, has written:

> *The subject of cultural difference becomes a problem that Walter Benjamin has described as the irresolution, or liminality, of "translation," the element of resistance in the process of transformation, "that element in a translation which does not lend itself to translation." This space of the translation of cultural difference at the interstices is infused with that Benjaminian temporality of the present which makes graphic a moment of transition . . .*[1]

1 Homi Bhabha, *The Location of Culture* (London: Routledge, 2004 [1994]), 321.

In other words, it is the incommensurability, that cultural difference between objects precisely that makes translation impossible, that makes approximate translation so powerful: like Brecht's epic theater, it makes visible its own chance and transformation in a process of pedagogical becoming. So, in this sense, approximate translation might be something that exists for all forms of translation—but, for our purposes, it is particularly valuable in this volume and in this context as a frame through which we can understand what exactly we are doing in urban design when we concoct designs and plans, translating one thing from the present to another thing in the future, or translating something from one place to another and back again, or when we move something from a medium like a historical narrative into another medium like the experiential, scripted, and built environment.

Approximate translation is the cipher, if you will, that can help you solve the riddles of urban design. Remembering this, we can apply it to all of the lessons imparted throughout this volume. One, the works of Marshall McLuhan, Sylvia Lavin, and Shannon Mattern remind us that cities and the built environment are media, and they can be designed and engaged with as such. When we design urban spaces, we not only draw lines that represent concrete sidewalks, asphalt streets, building massing, and open spaces. We also create surfaces, infrastructures, and systems for mediation. The urban plan mediates from the ideal form of an urban design to the actual built thing, but the built urban space also mediates between people, between people and systems, and between all kinds of communicative media: billboards, projections, sounds, smells, and beyond. In this sense, urban design is approximate translation between mediums. To be an urban designer is to be a media theorist, critic, and designer, and you can either work with intentionality or you can ignore this charge and reap the consequences. This is even true for conventional practices of urban design, like network and figure-ground analysis and intervention, where one takes the meaning inscribed in space and translates it to diagram form and back again—the urban design practices we began with in our design for Allston. To do so with an eye attuned to media only improves the process. More importantly, to be attuned to media is to be attuned to people. Urban design ultimately mediates people's relationship to each other and to space—designing for people is the most important thing of all.

Opposite page: Photos of visitors to Disneyland, taken by the author while conducting interviews. Source: author.

Two, theme parks, for all their faults, for all the accurate critiques lobbed by thinkers such as Michael Sorkin, that they take our publicness and replace it with corporatized and privatized banality, that they reduce our civic imagination to a space of consumption controlled by media empires, I argue that they can also be understood as media structures and used as such in the process of urban design. We can learn a lot from how Disney translates a film franchise into an immersive ride and back again, how media are used to engage the whole human sensorium. The basic ideas of urban design: organization of space, of connecting networks, of creating delightful spaces for people to exist within, of making meaningful spaces that draw from narrative, from history, and from our own desires that we ourselves project. There is no reason why these kinds of spaces—which are, at their essence, urban in the way that they bring multitudes of difference together in a collective form of dreaming—can't be designed for the public sphere and in the public interest.

Three, place-embedded histories are critical in the process of urban design. Translating these stories of place into urban plans for the future is a critical process, and one that goes too often overlooked with complaints of resulting urban spaces without consideration of place-embedded histories often sounding mysteriously similar: "this new neighborhood is dead, it has no soul, I don't feel like I belong here anymore." Important for this process of translation is an understanding of narrative: Hayden White's ideas on the practical past and metanarrative here are instructive, namely, that the urban designer can meaningfully create and insert micronarratives as well as structures for others to narrate their own stories, such that places retain the histories that make them the urban places that they are. To create a narrative, try beginning with analysis of a story's characters, events, and places. And go from there. In our example, we uncovered endlessly fascinating histories and narratives within Allston, a neighborhood that so many have looked past without a second thought, from its history with the first car dealership to its ongoing saga with Harvard and the old railyard—and just about every place that exists has their own unique histories, stories, and practical pasts.

Four, on the subject of narrative, there are other layers yet to consider. For narratives themselves can be translated, but also their internal structures can be manipulated, translated, geometrically transformed. Two processes that we have discussed that are ripe for use in urban design approximate translation are, first, displacement. In line with alienation and defamiliarization, these strategies involve removing the contextual elements that make a narrative—or place—familiar, placing a design, for example, in an unexpected site, to see what we can learn. They are strategies used in narrative to create cognitive shock within a reader, and so too do we need to shock ourselves out of comfortable familiarity in the process of urban design such that we can learn what is really important for a place. In this volume, we took Allston and dropped it into Hong Kong (not to mention, turned it into a theme park called Allstonland using place-based histories and theme park media structures) and learned much from the process. Second, and equally important, is to replace and reconstruct what we have displaced after this process of learning, for which an understanding of deconstruction and deconstructivism is also instructive. Here we took Allstonland and returned it back into Boston in the form of New Allston, bringing with it all that we learned from its displacement.

Five, to emphasize what we discussed earlier, reconstruction is as important as deconstruction. For all the theoretical power that the linguistic turn provided intellectuals, artists, and designers, it was often mistook for an end rather than a means. Deconstruction and displacement can be very powerful tools indeed for breaking something apart and understanding it better. But when it comes to designing for people, for leaving the world better off than how you found it, reconstruction is just the thing. And for urban designers, this process of approximate translation can look something like taking the abstract information that you learn, considering what this might mean for something in its ideal form—that is to say, as a perfect conceptual idea—and then to materialize that using form and function. Or, if you like, megaform and mediated program. And this was the essence of New Allston: six ideal forms (The Circle, The Square, The Line, The Curve, The Arrow, and The Polyline) transformed into real proposals for Allston, all of which operate as a megaform programmed with function, media, and most of all, an openness for change, for unexpected use, for the future.

Six, embrace the delirious. In other words, as mentioned previously, urban designers must consider a kind of openness in their designs, must avoid overprogramming or overdetermining a design such that it becomes unusable for people in its restriction. This was the magic of the Commissioners' Plan of 1811 for New York City, giving Manhattan the limitless possibility found within its gridiron street plan. And this is the magic of the Angeleno strip mall, giving a similar infinite possibility of use, misuse, and incongruity within its humble stucco walls. It is not uncommon for a designer to feel as though they must continue work until every last square inch, pixel, or detail is worked out fully; but as Rittel and Webber knew, design doesn't really have any inherent stopping point, and in fact I suggest that good design actually ought to leave something a little open-ended.[2] In this sense, our ideal forms of New Allston are just that: structural ideas just waiting to be filled with the messy material of reality, whether they are reprogrammable spaces filled in with a pop-up business or open lots on The Curve, waiting to be filled with a residential unit for an idiosyncratic family that we couldn't have ever expected.

And, finally, seven, don't underestimate the power of art in imparting new techniques, technologies, and ideas for use in the practice of urban design. Throughout this volume, we've looked at, among other things, projected video art (Pipilotti Rist), Pop (consider, for example the work of Dara Birnbaum), Surrealist practices (from the original artists who used the term, like André Breton and Salvador Dalí, but also from Pop Surrealists like Gary Baseman), and alter-histories (to use my term, including Nomeda and Gediminas Urbonas, and Christian Philipp Müller). Each offers ideas, tools, and new ways of seeing the world that can be very useful for urban designers. As one example, taking the synthesis of high and low that pop art offers allows us to see the value in the strip mall. Moreover, the tools used by Surrealism (mining the unconscious to layer conflicting narratives and elements) and by alter-histories (developing practical micronarratives, embedding them into urban designs) are especially important. For Allston, we surrealized New Allston into the form of a live model, using these techniques.

In all, I hope to leave you as either an urban designer with several new tools in your toolkit, or as a denizen of this world with a new perspective and appreciation for the collective space of our contemporary urban lives, not least of all including theme parks, strip malls, and nightlife—or, even better, perhaps you are now both.

2 Horst W. J. Rittel and Melvin M. Webber, "Dilemmas in a General Theory of Planning," *Policy Sciences* 4 (1973): 155–169, https://doi.org/10.1007/BF01405730..

Coda: Considering the Work of Lynn Xu

As I wrap up writing this book, I think of another artist that I recently encountered whose work seems relevant to the ideas we've explored. Lynn Xu is a poet and translator whose work exemplifies ideas from surrealism and the strip mall. She leaves open moments of ambiguity in her text that allow us to enter in, swirl with our subconscious, avoid overdetermination. They generate a kind of delirious quality: within this poem, one thinks, is a multitude of poems.

In one recent book-length poem, titled *And Those Ashen Heaps That Cantilevered Vase of Moonlight*, she works with approximate translation on multiple levels.[3] Within the poem itself, there is obvious translation between English and Chinese, couplets that stand alone on a page. The poem, written in juxtaposition of Xu's reflections on becoming a mother and her own mother, holds resonances and echoes of these ideas, though it would be a shallow interpretation to say that this is what the poem is about. One of these couplets:

to be born
出生

3 Lynn Xu, *And Those Ashen Heaps That Cantilevered Vase of Moonlight* (Seattle: Wave Books, 2022).

It is, on its face, a direct translation of some simple text from one language to another. But what are the limits of language? What is lost or gained in translation? Or, perhaps better: how can we observe transformation occur? Other translations occur within languages and at the edges of our comprehension. Xu plays with meaning and syntax in a way that is somehow similar to Chomsky's suggestion of a "grammatical" sentence that is not "meaningful":

Colorless green ideas sleep furiously.[4]

4 Noam Chomsky, *Syntactic Structures* (Berlin: Mouton de Gruyter, 2002 [1957]), 15.

What Chomsky hints at though doesn't focus on is the way our brains can take on a "grammatical but not meaningful" sentence or phrase and make meaning of it. It is the paranoiac-critical method that is always at work in our minds. And, indeed, this is true too for Xu's work, where her use and misuse of language is a spark that generates new meaning; it is a translation from English in the present into English in the future, as in the first three lines and their invention, their affective hint of new birth, of creation:

Rippling in the ceosops
foreskin of wind
still surrounded by blood

And there is a third layer yet of Xu's translation. The pages of her book-length poem were translated from the page into physical space as they were installed into the Museum of Contemporary Art Tucson from November 4, 2022 to January 8, 2023. The words of the pages wound their way around the floor, around walls, around giant-scale pages hung from the ceiling, hung sheets that bounded back up toward the ceiling in a catenary curve (a nod toward the titular cantilever?), framed into light-blocking decals pasted to the museum's garage-door windows.

Another translation: the spoken word of Xu's voice, in readings of the poem, in a reading that echoed through the cavernous space of MOCA Tucson becoming somehow more physical, in a conversation with me and Laura Copelin, MOCA's curator—all translations rippling out, each holding their own meaning while refracting the meaning found in their siblings and in the original. These all demonstrate so much of the essence of approximate translation in their move from one medium to another, to have the audacity to physicalize the written word and the spoken word—words that from their inception were surreal, poetic, dreamings of a poet and her readers.

Xu's poetry is a kind of urban design, lines on a page that are translated into sound, space, and experience, lines on a page that create, structure, and mediate experiences between people—at least for a time in Tucson, or perhaps at a reading or on Zoom, or even, perhaps, these lines mediate an experience between ourselves, between our conscious and unconscious mind as we read on our own and dream of a future.

The pages of Lynn Xu's poem translated into the glass panels of MOCA's roll-up walls. Source: author.

Bibliography

Avermaete, Tom, Fransje Hooimeijer, Lara Schrijver, eds. "Urban Formation and Collective Spaces." Special issue, *OASE* 71 (2006).

Baker, Carissa. "The Prevalence of Storyworlds and Thematic Landscapes in Global Theme Parks." *Annals of Tourism Research Empirical Insights* 4, no. 1 (2023): 1–10. https://doi.org/10.1016/j.annale.2022.100080.

Banham, Reyner. *Megastructure: Urban Futures of the Recent Past*. London: Thames and Hudson, 1976.

Bargh, John A., and Ezequiel Morsella. "The Unconscious Mind." *Perspectives on Psychological Science* 3, no. 1 (2008): 73–79. https://doi.org/10.1111/j.1745-6916.2008.00064.x.

Benjamin, Walter. "Theses on the Philosophy of History." In *Illuminations*, 253–264. New York: Harcourt, Brace & World, 1968.

Berlant, Lauren. *The Female Complaint: The Unfinished Business of Sentimentality in American Culture*. Durham: Duke University Press, 2008.

Bhabha, Homi. *The Location of Culture*. London: Routledge, 1994.

Bourriaud, Nicholas. "Public Relations." Interview by Bennett Simpson. *ArtForum*, April 2001.

Brecht, Bertold. "Alienation Effects in Chinese Acting." In *Brecht on Theater: The Development of an Aesthetic*, ed. John Willett, 91–99. New York: Hill and Wang, 1964.

Breton, André. *Manifestoes of Surrealism*. Ann Arbor: University of Michigan Press, 1969.

brown, adrienne maree. *Emergent Strategy: Shaping Change, Shaping Worlds*. Chico: AK Press, 2017.

Carmona, Matthew. *Public Places Urban Spaces: The Dimensions of Urban Design*. London: Routledge, 2010.

Carruthers, Peter. *The Opacity of Mind: An Integrative Theory of Self-Knowledge*. Oxford: Oxford University Press, 2011.

Chase, John, Margaret Crawford, and John Kaliski. *Everyday Urbanism*. New York: The Monacelli Press, 1999.

Chiu, Rebecca L. H. "Socio-Cultural Sustainability of Housing: A Conceptual Exploration." *Housing, Theory and Society* 21, no. 2 (2004): 65–76. https://doi.org/10.1080/14036090410014999.

Cho, Hyunjung. "Kenzō Tange's A Plan for Tokyo, 1960: A Plan for Urban Mobility." *arq* 22, no. 2 (2018): 139–150. https://doi.org/10.1017/S1359135518000301.

Choi, Wing Yee Kimburley. "Remade in Hong Kong: How Hong Kong People Use Hong Kong Disneyland." PhD thesis, Lingnan University, 2007. https://doi.org/10.14793/cs_etd.6.

Chomsky, Noam. *Syntactic Structures*. Berlin: Mouton de Gruyter, 1957.

Clavé, Salvador Anton. *The Global Theme Park Industry*. Wallingford: CABI, 2011.

Crisman, Jonathan Jae-an, Alycia Cheng, and Annette Kim. "From Shopping Centers to Cultural Centers: Los Angeles Strip Malls as Sites of Ethnic and Immigrant Placemaking." *Urban Geography*, published ahead of print (2024): 1–31. https://doi.org/10.1080/02723638.2024.2337569.

Crisman, Jonathan Jae-an. "Art and the Aesthetics of Cultural Gentrification: The Cases of Boyle Heights and Little Tokyo in Los Angeles." In *Aesthetics of Gentrification: Seductive Spaces and Exclusive Communities in the Neoliberal City*, ed. Christoph Lindner and Gerardo Sandoval, 137–154. Amsterdam: Amsterdam University Press, 2021. https://doi.org/10.1515/9789048551170-008.

Crisman, Jonathan Jae-an. "Practicing the Future: Exercises in Immanent Speculation." *Boom: A Journal of California* 6, no. 3 (2016): 25–31. https://doi.org/10.1525/boom.2016.6.3.25.

Crisman, Jonathan Jae-an, ed. "Socio–." Special issue, *Thresholds* 40 (2012).

Cuff, Dana, Anastasia Loukaitou-Sideris, Todd Presner, Maite Zubiaurre, and Jonathan Jae-an Crisman. *Urban Humanities: New Practices for Reimagining the City.* Cambridge: MIT Press, 2020.

Cupers, Kenny, and Markus Miessen. "Participation and/or Criticality? Thoughts on an Architectural Practice for Urban Change." In "Socio–," ed. Jonathan Crisman, special issue, *Thresholds* 40 (2012): 105–112. https://doi.org/10.1162/thld_a_00138.

Custers, Ruud, and Henk Aarts. "The Unconscious Will: How the Pursuit of Goals Operates Outside of Conscious Awareness." *Science* 329, no. 5987 (2010): 47–50. https://doi.org/10.1126/science.1188595.

Davis, Mike. *City of Quartz: Excavating the Future in Los Angeles.* London: Verso, 1990.

de Certeau, Michel. *The Practice of Everyday Life.* Berkeley: The University of California Press, 1984.

Derrida, Jacques. *Of Grammatology.* Baltimore: Johns Hopkins University Press, 1976.

Derrida, Jacques, and Peter Eisenman. *Chora L Works.* New York: Monacelli Press, 1997.

d'Hoine, Pieter, and Marije Martijn, eds. *All From One: A Guide to Proclus.* Oxford: Oxford University Press, 2017.

Drigas, Athanasios, and Eleni Mitsea. "The 8 Pillars of Metacognition." *International Journal of Emerging Technologies in Learning (iJET)* 15, no. 21 (2020): 162–178. https://doi.org/10.3991/ijet.v15i21.14907.

Dunne, Anthony, and Fiona Raby. *Speculative Everything: Design, Fiction, and Social Dreaming.* Cambridge: MIT Press, 2013.

Edelheim, Johan R. *Tourist Attractions: From Object to Narrative.* Bristol: Channel View Publications, 2016.

Frampton, Kenneth. "Megaform as Urban Landscape." *Journal of Delta Urbanism* 2 (2021): 14–23.

Frenchman, Dennis. "Event-Places in North America: City Meaning and Making." *Places* 16, no. 3 (2004): 36–49.

Global Industry Analysts, Inc. *Amusement and Theme Parks: A Global Strategic Business Report.* San Jose: Global Industry Analysts, Inc., 2023.

Guberman, Marc, Jacob Reidel, and Frida Rosenberg, eds. "Monster." Special issue, *Perspecta* 40 (2008).

Hara, Kenya. *Designing Design.* Baden: Lars Muller, 2011.

Hillier, Bill. *Space Is the Machine: A Configurational Theory of Architecture.* London: Space Syntax, 1996.

Holmes, James S. "The Name and Nature of Translation Studies." In *Translated! Papers on Literary Translation and Translation Studies*, 67–80. Amsterdam: Rodopi, 1988.

Horkheimer, Max, and Theodor W. Adorno. "The Culture Industry: Enlightenment as Mass Deception." In *Dialectic of Enlightenment*, 120–167. New York: Herder and Herder, 1972.

Hussein, Fatmaelzahraa, John Stephens, and Reena Tiwari. "Cultural Memories and Sense of Place in Historic Urban Landscapes: The Case of Masrah Al Salam, the Demolished Theatre Context in Alexandria, Egypt." *Land* 9, no. 8 (2020): 264. https://doi.org/10.3390/land9080264.

Institute for Art and Urban Resources. *This Is Tomorrow Today: The Independent Group and British Pop Art.* New York: Institute for Art and Urban Resources, 1987.

Jarzombek, Mark. "ECO-POP: In Praise of Irony, Hyperbole, and Readymades." *Cornell Journal of Architecture* 8 (2011): 58–62.

Jarzombek, Mark. *Urban Heterology: Dresden and the Dialectics of Post-Traumatic History.* Lund: Lund University, Department of Theoretical and Applied Aesthetics, 2001.

Jenkins, Henry. *Textual Poachers: Television Fans & Participatory Culture.* London: Routledge, 1992.

Johnson, Philip. *Mies van der Rohe.* New York: Museum of Modern Art, 1947.

Karnowsky, Merry. "Pop Surrealism at the Ends of the Earth." In *Apocalypse Wow! Pop Surrealism, Neo Pop, Urban Art*, ed. Julie Kogler and Giorgio Calcara. Milan: Silvana Editoriale, 2009.

King, Margaret J. "The Disney Effect: Fifty Years After Theme Park Design." In *Disneyland and Culture: Essays on the Parks and Their Influence*, ed. Kathy Merlock Jackson and Mark I. West, 223–226. Jefferson: McFarland, 2011.

Klein, Norman. *The Vatican to Vegas: A History of Special Effects.* New York: New Press, 2004.

Kogler, Julie, and Giorgio Calcara, eds. *Apocalypse Wow! Pop Surrealism, Neo Pop, Urban Art.* Milan: Silvana Editoriale, 2009.

Koolhaas, Rem. *Delirious New York: A Retroactive Manifesto for Manhattan.* New York: The Monacelli Press, 1997.

Koolhaas, Rem. "Junkspace." *October* 100 (2002): 175–190. https://doi.org/10.1162/016228702320218457.

Koolhaas, Rem. "Singapore Songlines: Portrait of a Potemkin Metropolis . . . or Thirty Years of Tabula Rasa." In *S,M,L,XL*, 1008–1089. New York: The Monacelli Press, 1995.

Koolhaas, Rem, and Hans Ulrich Obrist. *Project Japan: Metabolism Talks.* Koln: Taschen, 2012.

Kronfeld, Chana. *The Full Severity of Compassion: The Poetry of Yehuda Amichai.* Redwood City: Stanford University Press, 2016.

Kyriazi, Gary. *The Great American Amusement Parks.* Secaucus: Citadel Press, 1976.

Lavin, Sylvia. *Kissing Architecture.* Princeton: Princeton University Press, 2011.

Lin, Zhongjie. "Urban Structure for the Expanding Metropolis: Kenzo Tange's 1960 Plan for Tokyo." *Journal of Architectural and Planning Research* 24, no. 2 (2007): 109–124.

Linovski, Orly. "Beyond Aesthetics: Assessing the Value of Strip Mall Retail in Toronto." *Journal of Urban Design* 17, no. 1 (2012): 81–99. https://doi.org/10.1080/13574809.2011.646247.

Lipsitz, George. "The Racialization of Space and the Spatialization of Race: Theorizing the Hidden Architecture of Landscape." *Landscape Journal* 26, no. 1 (2007): 10–23.

Longstreth, Richard. *The Drive-in, the Supermarket, and the Transformation of Commercial Space in Los Angeles, 1914–1941.* Cambridge: MIT Press, 1999.

Loukaitou-Sideris, Anastasia. "Regeneration of Urban Commercial Strips: Ethnicity and Space in Three Los Angeles Neighborhoods." *Journal of Architectural and Planning Research* 19, no. 4 (2002): 334–350.

Lucas, Raymond, and Ombretta Romice. "Representing Sensory Experience in Urban Design." *Design Principles and Practices* 2, no. 4 (2008): 83–94. https://doi.org/10.18848/1833-1874/CGP/v02i04/37579.

Lui, Tai-Lok. "Beneath the Appearance of Gentrification: Probing Local Complexities." *International Journal of Urban and Regional Research* 41, no. 3 (2017): 478–486. https://doi.org/10.1111/1468-2427.12497.

Lukas, Scott A. *The Immersive Worlds Handbook: Designing Theme Parks and Consumer Spaces*. London: Routledge, 2019.

Lynch, Kevin. *A Theory of Good City Form*. Cambridge: MIT Press, 1981.

Lyotard, Jean-François. *The Postmodern Condition: A Report on Knowledge*. Minneapolis: University of Minnesota Press, 1984.

Mattern, Shannon. *Code and Clay, Data and Dirt: Five Thousand Years of Urban Media*. Minneapolis: University of Minnesota Press, 2017.

McLuhan, Marshall, and Quentin Fiore. *The Medium is the Massage: An Inventory of Effects*. New York: Bantam Books, 1967.

Molotch, Harvey. "The City as a Growth Machine: Toward a Political Economy of Place." *American Journal of Sociology* 82, no. 2 (1976): 309–332. https://doi.org/10.1086/226311.

Morton, Timothy. *Hyperobjects: Philosophy and Ecology after the End of the World*. Minneapolis: University of Minnesota Press, 2013.

Peterson, Mary A., and Emily Skow Grant. "Memory and Learning in Figure-Ground Perception." *Cognitive Vision: Psychology of Learning and Motivation* 42 (2003): 1–34. https://doi.org/10.1016/S0079-7421(03)01001-6.

Pistoni, Roberta, and Sophie Bonin. "Urban Metabolism Planning and Designing Approaches between Quantitative Analysis and Urban Landscape." *City, Territory and Architecture* 4, no. 1 (2017): 1–11. https://doi.org/10.1186/s40410-017-0076-y.

Porteous, John Douglas. "Home: The Territorial Core." *Geographical Review* 66, no. 4 (1976): 383–390. https://doi.org/10.2307/213649.

Proust, Joëlle. *The Philosophy of Metacognition: Mental Agency and Self-Awareness*. Oxford: Oxford University Press, 2013.

Punday, Daniel, *Narrative after Deconstruction*. Albany: SUNY Press, 2002.

Rams, Dieter. *Less but Better*. Germany: Jo Klatt Design + Design Verlag, 1995.

Redding, Gordon M., and Benjamin Wallace. "Adaptive Spatial Alignment and Strategic Perceptual-Motor Control." *Journal of Experimental Psychology: Human Perception and Performance* 22, no. 2 (1996): 379–94. https://doi.org/10.1037/0096-1523.22.2.379.

Rittel, Horst W. J., and Melvin M. Webber. "Dilemmas in a General Theory of Planning." *Policy Sciences* 4 (1973): 155–169. https://doi.org/10.1007/BF01405730.

Santander, Arturo Azpeitia, Agustín Azkarate Garai-Olaun, and Ander De la Fuente Arana. "Historic Urban Landscapes: A Review on Trends and Methodologies in the Urban Context of the 21st Century." *Sustainability* 10, no. 8 (2018): 2603. https://doi.org/10.3390/su10082603.

Schrijver, Lara. "Whatever Happened to Projective Architecture? Rethinking the Expertise of the Architect." *Footprint* 4 (2009): 123–127.

Shklovsky, Viktor. "Art as Technique." In *Russian Formalist Criticism: Four Essays*, 3–24. Lincoln: University of Nebraska Press, 1917.

Sitte, Camillo. *City Planning According to Artistic Principles*. New York: Random House, 1965.

Soja, Edward W. *Postmodern Geographies: The Reassertion of Space in Critical Social Theory*. London: Verso, 1989.

Somol, Robert, and Sarah Whiting. "Notes around the Doppler Effect and Other Moods of Modernism." *Perspecta* 33 (2002): 72–77.

Sorkin, Michael, ed. *Variations on a Theme Park: The New American City and the End of Public Space*. New York: The Noonday Press, 1992.

Topolovská, Tereza. "Reading Buildings: The Textual Turn of Architecture as a Parallel to the Spatial Turn in Literary Studies." *Ars Aeterna* 14, no. 1 (2022): 58–70. https://doi.org/10.2478/aa-2022-0006.

Varnelis, Kazys. "Conclusion: The Meaning of Network Culture." In *Networked Publics*, ed. Kazys Varnelis, 145–163. Cambridge: MIT Press, 2008.

Venturi, Robert, Denise Scott Brown, and Steven Izenour. *Learning from Las Vegas*. Cambridge: MIT Press, 1972.

Wark, McKenzie. *Raving*. Durham: Duke University Press, 2023.

Weir, Simon. "Salvador Dalí in Rem Koolhaas' Delirious New York." *The Journal of Architecture* 27, no. 2–3 (2022): 398–419. https://doi.org/10.1080/13602365.2022.2106580.

White, Hayden. *The Practical Past*. Evanston: Northwestern University Press, 2014.

Williams, Rebecca. *Theme Park Fandom: Spatial Transmedia, Materiality and Participatory Cultures*. Amsterdam: Amsterdam University Press, 2020.

Xu, Lynn. *And Those Ashen Heaps That Cantilevered Vase of Moonlight*. Seattle: Wave Books, 2022.

Yang, Yang, Yihong Li Katharina Kral, Nathaniel Hupert, and Timur Dogan. "Urban Design Attributes and Resilience: COVID-19 Evidence from New York City." *Buildings & Cities* 2, no. 1 (2021): 618–636. https://doi.org/10.5334/bc.130.

Young, Iris Marion. *Inclusion and Democracy*. Oxford: Oxford University Press, 2002.

Young, Iris Marion. "The Ideal of Community and the Politics of Difference." *Social Theory and Practice* 12, no. 1 (1986): 22.

Zadeh, Lotfi. "Fuzzy Sets." *Information and Control* 8 (1965): 338–353. https://doi.org/10.1016/S0019-9958(65)90241-X.

Zhou, Zhengnan, Lei Qu, and Tao Zou. "Quantitative Analysis of Urban Pluvial Flood Alleviation by Open Surface Water Systems in New Towns: Comparing Almere and Tianjin Eco-city." *Sustainability* 7, no. 10 (2015): 1-28. https://doi.org/10.3390/su71013378.

Acknowledgements

This book was somewhat of an unexpected project, resuscitating my thesis work from my time at MIT and reworking it based on more recent scholarship. It came about from my involvement with Erin and Ian Besler's book *Best Practices* where I encountered the wonderful people at AR+D—so thank you to the Beslers, and especially Jake Anderson at AR+D. Thanks are also due to Emily Merin and Aila Fe Teves who helped me get the book's contents in order. To my old MIT friends, teachers, and collaborators, especially including Mark Jarzombek, Nomeda and Gediminas Urbonas, Dennis Frenchman, Alexander D'Hooghe, and Nancy Kim: you were instrumental to the intellectual and creative ideas in this book. I was surrounded by so many wonderful people at MIT, including all the folks included in this book who were willing to respond to what was likely a bizarre request to help me fabricate imaginary Polaroids. And a special thanks to Annette Kim, who I followed from MIT in Boston to USC in Los Angeles, and who I continue to collaborate with—including ongoing work on our beloved strip malls. I would also like to thank my endlessly supportive and encouraging colleagues in the Department of Public and Applied Humanities at the University of Arizona. Lastly, thanks to my dear friend Ly Tran whose design wizardry elevated this book to what it is, my family for their love and support, and to John for everything.